More praise for Landon J. Napoleon

"Weird, funky, and offbeat—Landon J. Napoleon's writing is a harrowing, hysterical, and ultimately life-affirming romp through America's dark and desperate underbelly. His prose reads like you would imagine a road-rocker's elegy sounds—gritty, jagged, and full of passion."

—David S. Goyer
Writer/director of *Blade: Trinity*,
ZigZag, and writer of *Batman Begins*

"…an affecting work."

—*Dallas Morning News*

"Skillful wordplay and a strong sense of narrative timing. *ZigZag* is deserving of the advance praise."

—*Java Magazine*

"…like a portrait of Huck Finn in negative."

—*Sunday Times*
United Kingdom

"…a moving piece dealing with the issues of physical abuse and racism. Involving…"

—*Glasgow University Guardian*

"Landon J. Napoleon conveys the strength of the human spirit through his wonderful creation…an engaging and enriching story."

—*Barnes and Noble*
Discover Great
New Writers

The Spirit Warrior's Handbook

The Spirit Warrior's Handbook

✦

a practical guide to finding true freedom

Landon J. Napoleon

iUniverse, Inc.
New York Lincoln Shanghai

The Spirit Warrior's Handbook
a practical guide to finding true freedom

iUniverse books may be ordered through booksellers or by contacting:

iUniverse
2021 Pine Lake Road, Suite 100
Lincoln, NE 68512
www.iuniverse.com
1-800-Authors (1-800-288-4677)

ISBN: 0-595-33986-7

Printed in the United States of America

This book is dedicated to all my soul brothers from Wednesday morning and beyond—you know who you are—

and to each Spirit Warrior who has the courage to step on the path and look within.

Contents

PART III: Your return home

Acknowledgments

With deep appreciation and love to my own spirit guides without whom this book never would have materialized (alphabetically): Marcus Earle, Ralph Earle, Brenda Garrett, Deborah Stelzleni, and the other healers I've encountered on my path.

Heartfelt gratitude to my investor friends who made production of this book possible.

Special thanks to Jeffrey Moss at Moss Creative (mosscreative.com) who created a stunning cover at a reduced fee.

And, of course, eternal love and gratitude to Amy Lynn for being you and opening a door inside me that led to many of the spiritual epiphanies found herein.

Foreword

I met Landon four years ago on a Wednesday morning, early. I knew nothing of him nor the others attending the group meeting. We were eight strangers gathering to share our common fears and struggles, our unending tendency to turn to old patterns—alcohol, drugs, food, sex, workaholism—to cope with trauma, careers, relationships, marriage, fatherhood, life. Many of us also faced a mounting toll of seemingly-impossible circumstances. And so we began the meeting with Landon the first to speak. I was scared to death.

I knew that Landon must be an artist of some type. He looked way too hip to be among the ranks of lawyers, accountants, doctors and business professionals. Landon read from his journal. The man could obviously write. Turns out, many passages from those early journals would years later become the seeds for *The Spirit Warrior's Handbook*. I immediately admired him. I connected with his words.

From that Wednesday forward, we became increasingly good friends and forged bonds with the other men who regularly came to group. Over time, I gradually opened up to them. I shared my struggle, my pain, my loss, my sorrow, my shame. And so did they. We supported each other. We began a slow-but-steady healing from our respective traumas. Some of us worked the steps, others just talked and listened. Many came once or twice, or for a few months, and then continued on their path. A handful of us became regulars and through that process, brothers—or 'Spirit Warriors' as Landon came to call us—living to fight another day, to discover our own dormant potential.

I look back and realize that the Wednesday morning group had been a small miracle for me. The group literally saved my life. My new friends helped me face my demons. I found peace and stopped seeking the fleeting highs that I originally mistook for happiness.

Now, four years later, I see things more clearly. And what I see is many people facing the same struggles. People battling and losing. Not warriors, in the sense of summoning inner rather than external strength, nor spiritual in finding lasting peace and freedom. People unhappy. Slowly unraveling. Turning away from themselves and resorting to the many escapes available in our quick-fix society. *Need to shake depression?* Get a prescription. *Feel down?* Have a drink. *Tense?* Grab a smoke. *Low self-esteem?* Work without regard to family; shop without regard to true cost. *Overweight?* Starve on the latest fad diet, or worse, staple your stomach. *Unhappy?* Place a bet at the nearest casino. *Tension at home?* Start a fling with someone new. Find a compulsion; they're everywhere.

One truth I've learned: we all escape. We all check out. It's those of us who lose control over our methods of coping who slide even further into darkness and despair. I've been there. I've seen it countless times. I see it in movies, observe it among friends and professional peers, and hear it in songs. Maybe you do too. The lyrics from a song I frequently turned to during my journey, from Belgian band *K's Choice*, capture our common struggle:

> *Breathe it in and breathe it out*
> *And pass it on, it's almost out*
> *We're so creative, so much more*
> *We're high above but on the floor*
>
> *It's not a habit, it's cool I feel alive*
> *If you don't have it you're on the other side*
>
> *The deeper you stick it in your vein*
> *The deeper the thoughts, there's no more pain*
> *I am in heaven, I am a god*
> *I am everywhere, I feel so hot*
>
> *It's not a habit, it's cool I feel alive*
> *If you don't have it you're on the other side*
> *I am not an addict...*
> *Maybe, that's a lie.*

With the help of my brothers from Wednesday mornings, I discovered I was becoming a Spirit Warrior, that I had incredible hidden power to cope. I just never tapped it. The strength was buried deep in a part of me I never explored. Indeed, I had the makings to seek healthy change. The lesson I learned is that sometimes change really means no change at all. As you will learn in this book, it means allowing you to be yourself. Let yourself be, and growth will come. Your authentic Self will emerge if you let it breathe. Stop the constant change, stop being perfect. Stop searching for something better—be happy with what you have. Just live. Fail. Cry. Eat. Breathe. Open your eyes. Live. Simple words, but life's lessons abound.

So, savor the pages that follow. *The Spirit Warrior's Handbook* contains all the lessons you will ever need from someone I've watched walk the path. I'm hopeful that, as they did for me, Landon's words will help you find your own small miracle.

—Brian, a Wednesday morning brother
December 2004

When you step into Self
And see, for the first time,
That the search is over
Your mind will ask, "Over?"
And your soul will smile and answer
With silence.

Introduction

You are going to become a Spirit Warrior.

Welcome to the tribe. Man or woman, you have already begun the greatest journey you will ever undertake: discovering, knowing and, ultimately, embracing your true Self. And in your triumph you will finally escape the grip of that gnawing voice of fear and anxiety that has convinced you of its most crushing lie: that you're not good enough.

The freedom you seek is real and will wrap you in the warm glow of unconditional love. You are exactly where you should be at this moment, for you are on the path. Rest easy, for everything has already changed. Are you ready to believe that?

Do not be misguided. This book does not hold any of the answers you seek. There are no magic formulas contained herein nor is this book yet-another dogma or set of rules or lessons that will give you the missing talisman to your freedom puzzle. No book or person or anything outside you has the answers. Who you are and who you will become are choices and responsibilities that are solely yours.

This book is simply another tool that might help you uncover the freedom you already know. Consider the following truth and what it can tell you about the place you seek within yourself:

> *The touch point of your life is a drop in the Ocean of Eternity,*
> *and eternity is who you are.*

As a Spirit Warrior you are joining an ancient and sacred tribe of truth seekers. You become a Spirit Warrior simply by stepping on the path. Man or woman, you are now a warrior. Not in the sense of conquering life or others or your own demons through force or sheer will, but rather by shifting your focus inward and finding your highest and best.

Being a Spirit Warrior is about peace, not war. You find peace by merging all your feminine and masculine energies and returning to the wholeness you are. Man or woman, you become a Spirit Warrior by embracing your spirit energies—creativity, tenderness, love, intuition, spontaneity—with your warrior energies—power, strength, decisiveness, stability, fearlessness—as the basis for your transformation.

A Spirit Warrior does not adopt a new creed or allegiance to any particular dogma. Whatever level of spiritual faith you already practice or don't practice is perfect. Being a Spirit Warrior works in unity with wherever you are spiritually. Non-believers, believers and everyone in between all face the same journey to lasting inner peace. You do not have to change or abandon anything you are already doing. You simply have to be willing to become aware and let go of what you believe to be real. Everything is about to change.

The realm of the Spirit Warrior is the infinite. There is no organized structure or hierarchy. There are no buildings, monuments, idols or any other institutional markers. There are no commandments or punishments nor prescribed rituals. You will find no membership roles, no dues, and no official HOW TO literature of any kind. There are no meetings to attend, Sunday morning services, pre-scribed holidays or planned events. This book does not even purport to have the answers. You are entering the world of the unseen spirit where you author your own sacred text upon your heart. This is your solo voyage to the unknown and the unseen. This is your journey into the void. This is your journey home, Spirit Warrior.

Your strength and power come not from control or brute force; your strength is in laying down the arms of the past and picking up spiritual weaponry. Accep-tance. Surrender. Trust. Humility is your new shield.

From your confident warrior self, you do not need anyone's permission to be who you truly are. To be your best. Like a warrior, your actions are true and deci-sive. You speak your truth without fear because you are already free. And you forge your freedom by facing the inner fires of your pain and then extinguishing those flames with the cool waters of truth.

Whether you are struggling through the darkness of powerful addiction pat-terns or just want to finally lose that weight or have a better relationship with your partner, the Spirit Warrior path will prove vital. The journey is the same for us all. You will rediscover your true Self, that seed of possibility inside you per-haps dormant for many years and yet infinitely patient in awaiting your return. In other words, what you seek is already inside you.

The lessons in this book are simply another way to lead you to the doors of your own knowing. Ultimately, you will still have to pull open those great doors of discovery and embrace your truth. And within your truth awaits your freedom.

Finally, *The Spirit Warrior's Handbook* is not a novel to buzz through in three sittings and put back on the shelf. The text is not lengthy, but it is concentrated.

There are many questions to ponder. There are exercises to help you find your own answers. So please take your time. Read a lesson and then put the book down. Then take a few days, or even a week or more, to ponder and formulate your own answers to the questions presented. Record your thoughts, dreams and discoveries on a notepad or in a journal. Indeed, this is not a passive read for entertainment; this is a text that will ask you to take off your mask and do your inner work. Surrender. Discipline. Patience. Gentleness. Taking action. These are all Spirit Warrior traits that you can begin honing simply by how you approach this text. Pick up the torch of your own freedom by giving yourself the gift of real transformation. Spend a month or two, or even longer, working your way through this text.

You are ready to begin. The tribe is gathered to greet you, to support you, to send you on your journey. The drumbeat of celebration is in the air. The dance has begun. The sun and moon and stars are aligned for you. It is time. You are ready to give yourself the deep connection and joy you deserve. You are ready for ultimate freedom. As you begin your journey, doubt and fear are good signs because you are expanding old comfort zones.

Begin your journey anyway.

You are going to become a Spirit Warrior.

A note from the author

The bulk of this book began as passages, ideas, random entries, and epiphanies from the author's handwritten journals beginning in February 1999. A novelist the first time out, it was never the author's intention to write a non-fiction, personal growth book. Rather, the book revealed itself in hindsight, years later, as part of the author's own healing journey. May you, too, find your freedom and everlasting peace in your own unique way.

PART I

Your cosmic journey begins

1

Love yourself.

Spirit Warrior, let go of trying to control life.
Instead, you now find your new power in acceptance and surrender.

Your heroic mission starts where everything worthwhile begins and ends: love. The first and most important truth is also one of the most difficult. Your ego will tell you this love stuff is nonsense and, if anything, should come at the end of your warrior training after you've had a chance to revamp your life and stack up some successes. But love yourself right now? Most likely, your ego will scream in protest that this is ludicrous and impossible.

As a Spirit Warrior, you now begin to identify that voice of doubt and fear as nothing more than the incessant rambling of ego. The ego is just an idea in your mind, an illusion, a lie that you are separate from everything: other people, nature, and all that is Divine. The ego's job is to keep you separate, which is to keep you safe. The ego's Big Lie is that you are not good enough, and all the other lies spin-off from there. Since you're not good enough, you're also unworthy and unlovable and therefore don't deserve good things in life. If this sounds familiar, you're not alone. All humans are susceptible to believing the lies in their own minds.

The ego voice controls you through fear, shame and guilt. And sadly, the voice has been present for so long we understandably mistake the voice as truth. We believe it not because it's truth, but because it's been talking as far back as we can remember.

The ego voice keeps you in fear by operating on a cause-and-effect approach to self-love and acceptance that says, *You'll never be enough, but if you achieve, acquire, buy, and own A-B-C-D, you'll get closer....*

But we do not get closer, we only get tired from running to the next external thing that someone says will finally make us feel okay inside. It's a set-up and a revolving cycle that only reinforces the lies. And the more you reinforce lies, the more you believe and act upon them. Even when you are able to check one or two or ten things off the list, the ego presents you with more demands. *You must have got lucky there,* the ego whispers, and *now once you do this, this, this and that, then maybe we'll see about this love-yourself nonsense.*

Following the dictates of the ego's fundamental lie that you're not good enough only brings more agony and anxiety because feeding the ego strengthens it and leads you further from the truth. Ponder the truth below and see if you can just be open to the possibility without judging it as true or false.

Spirit Warrior, you were born into the tribe perfect and whole.
Your quest is to return to that truth and embrace who you have always been.

Regardless of what you do or how much you accomplish or how much money you have, you will never fill the void or erase the emptiness you feel or find the security you seek with something outside yourself. Ask yourself, does that voice in your head ever stop regardless of what you do? The answer for most of us, before we transcend our old ways, is *NO, NEVER, NO MATTER WHAT I DO!* That should be a good clue that nothing external will bring peace if you can't simply love yourself right now, one hundred percent, without any reservations or conditions.

Perhaps most tragic are the people, both the famous and the unknown, who do manage to fulfill the ego's impossible dictates and align the long list of externals—physical beauty, accolades and trophies, the Barbie or Ken spouse, the monetary fortune—and then kill themselves. What they couldn't find outside is what we all crave and need inside: self-love and acceptance. The ego's promises are nothing but lies, and the lies always leave us feeling empty and lonely. It usually requires a personal meltdown, a crisis, a near-death experience or some other tragedy that snaps us out of our trance. The ego is a cruel master to follow.

A fear of one's own greatness and intimacy
Drives many to madness.
Running, searching, terrified to pause
And look within.
When one finally stops and pulls back to breathe
The infinite truth suffuses Being
And Being, one realizes,
Is living in greatness and intimacy
With Self and others.
To love and be loved; that is all.
The search ends not on the highest mountain

Or in the arms of a new lover or in the illusion
Of a new drug.
But rather, quietly, in the space of aloneness
Where Love has been patiently waiting
For all time.

As a Spirit Warrior, you are turning away from ego thinking. Under the illusion of the ego, you'll *never* be good enough or worthy of love and certainly not deserving of your own self-acceptance and love. *Never.*

Your new power comes not from destroying the ego. Instead, you treat the ego as you would a child acting out for attention. You no longer give the Big Lie your attention, and eventually the child (ego) gives up because you're no longer playing its game. You do this by allowing the ego to chatter away about how this self-love stuff is nonsense, and you begin to love yourself regardless. In fact, you don't have to fix your flaws and brokenness to be okay. You're already okay right now. And you certainly don't need anyone's approval to love yourself right now. Even if your ego is balking, keep reading.

Spirit Warrior,
how might your life begin to change if you chose to love and accept yourself
as you would a newborn baby to the tribe?

Ultimately, loving yourself is simply a choice you make and, although it's easy to get swept up in the myth, has no connection to how many external trophies or how much money you stack up or how attractive you or your partner may be physically.

As a Spirit Warrior, you now simply choose not to enter any battle that is impossible to win. Victory is gained without ever setting foot on the battlefield; the ego has no defense if you do not engage in the fight. When you don't show up for the fight, the war ends before the war can ever begin. The Big Lie in your head, that you're not good enough, loses power each time you choose to let it be. That is, you can let the voice ramble without giving it any importance. Try this or some version of the same that works for you: *I hear you, and I don't believe what you're telling me. I know I'm good enough and lovable, and I'm not going to act on your lies anymore. I'm on a new path now.*

This is the beginning of your new foundation, which you build from the inside. You begin by replacing fear and shame and guilt with love and acceptance. You start in this moment by loving yourself regardless of where you are or what you have in your bank account and no matter how low you believe you have sunk. If you have enough energy to read these words, you have the power to change no matter how loud your ego screams *Love myself! Are you crazy? Here are the reasons I can't love myself...*And away your ego goes. The ego in action is like a dog wrestling with a toy. Just let the dog be and eventually it will wear itself out and stop. You can simply observe the process without getting caught up in trying to stop or fight what's happening. Paradoxically, the less you do in this arena, the more quickly the situation resolves itself.

Loving yourself has nothing to do with arrogance or conceit; loving yourself simply means you stop berating yourself for never measuring up to some false image of what you should be.

> *Spirit Warrior, go outside right now and look to the sky...*
> *And take a long, deep breath.*
> *Smile.*
> *It's okay.*
> *It's time to ease up on yourself.*
> *Just breathe and let go for a few minutes.*
> *And then listen to what the clouds and stars and moon can teach you about accepting*
> *who you are right now: your strengths and weaknesses, your triumphs and mistakes,*
> *your hopes, dreams and fears.*

Make this sky gazing a new Spirit Warrior habit and see what you learn about acceptance and love. As a Spirit Warrior, today begins the journey of learning to love yourself unconditionally. Whether the lesson comes first or last or ten years from now, you will still have to make the choice to love yourself in spite of your human flaws, in spite of the many mistakes you've made, and regardless of the ego's stern warnings and protests. Welcome to the tribe.

It is time. The power to change your life is always right now. Not tonight or tomorrow or next week. As a Spirit Warrior you do not hesitate to act. You probably wouldn't be reading these words unless you've been getting ready to love yourself for a long time. How do you start?

First, breathe deep.

Then breathe deep again and let go of that impossible list of things you tell yourself you have to do and accomplish to finally be okay. Just mentally set the list aside (it won't go anywhere) and be with yourself minus all the demands. Read the following affirmations slowly several times and feel what you already know to be real, but perhaps you've forgotten.

*I am love. I am peace.
I am spirit.*

What if in this moment, just to try a different approach, you chose to start treating yourself with the unconditional love, acceptance and tenderness you would give that newborn infant to the tribe? You can always go back to the old way, but what about easing that harsh grip just for this moment? What if you gave yourself kind words of acceptance and soothing encouragement rather than cruelly berating that little child who's only trying to learn? How about just telling yourself right now that you already measure up and that everything's going to be okay? What if you just reminded yourself that it's okay to be afraid and that no matter what, I LOVE YOU? And then you said all those things again and again. Not just once or twice or ten times, but hundreds of times a day. Many of us have spent years telling ourselves hundreds of times a day that we're no good, and we know how that feels. Are you willing to try something new?

As Spirit Warriors, we use that same technique of repetition to remind ourselves how good we already are. And we do it over and over and over just like a parent soothing a child startled awake by a bad dream. All that child needs is your love and to feel safe. That's all.

*It's okay to be scared. I'm here for you,
and I love you no matter what. It's okay to cry.
I love you. I'm here for you. You're going to be okay.*

This approach may definitely trigger your ego's fear and disapproval as nothing but New Age nonsense. The ego voice may scream quite loudly that affirmations are a waste of time and don't work. Your mind may even start to believe what it's hearing. That's okay. Just let the voices ramble without entering the fight.

In truth, there's actually no dispute that affirmations, usually negative and self-critical ones, work very well. Try this: Stop for a moment and observe in your mind, without judging anything, every thing and every relationship in your life right now. This is the reality you have created because you can only create what you act upon. Going back another step, your actions are always preceded by a thought: *I want cookie dough ice cream.* It would be impossible to find yourself spontaneously eating cookie dough ice cream without first having the thought to do so.

All actions, therefore, begin in the mind as thoughts, or affirmations, we repeat over and over to ourselves. Through repetition, those affirmations become beliefs that dictate our choices because we choose based on what we believe is possible for ourselves. This cycle—thought/affirmation, action, reality—has created the results you see in your own life right now. What we believe about ourselves, what we *affirm* in our minds, has to become our reality. If what we affirm to ourselves is harsh and critical, we become fearful and anxious and perhaps even immobilized. We have problems in our relationships and keep attracting the same type of partners. We never seem to quite get ahead of the bills. We act out our fears and shame with self-destructive habits and patterns. We disconnect. We cry out to be loved and then, out of fear, push that very love away. Whatever our reality, it all begins in the unseen dimension of the mind with what we tell ourselves over and over again. Every thought becomes a seed for our future.

All you're doing now, as a Spirit Warrior, is taking what you can see already works and changing the chant you play in your head to one of truth and evolution. Learning to love and accept yourself is interwoven with your ability to create the life you want. You cannot generate inner feelings of worthiness if you do not accept yourself. You cannot feel truly deserving of success if you do not love yourself. Everything begins with you and your thoughts/affirmations and beliefs that you are worthy and deserving.

This lesson comes first because to change any outer behavior patterns you must begin at the core. And the inner core of becoming a Spirit Warrior is one hundred percent self-love and acceptance. Let us not delay; go to the mirror, look yourself in the eyes as you would that small child and simply say, "I love and accept myself exactly as I am."

If that is too painful or difficult, start with "I am willing to let go and accept things the way they are." If that is too painful or difficult, try "I am willing to learn new things."

Keep going until you find your surrender opening. Maybe it's just, "I am willing." Or maybe it's not saying anything. Just look into your eyes and smile and reconnect with that perfect, loving part of yourself that is pure spirit. Don't be surprised if you start to cry when you do this. The moment we stop running and have the courage to look at and be with ourselves is very powerful.

Have fun and play with this idea. Love yourself for all the silly things you've done. Love yourself for all the wonderful things you've done. Love yourself for all the things you never quite got around to doing. Love yourself for having the courage to be on this path of discovering new parts of yourself. Love yourself for the painful lessons you repeated over and over. Love yourself for repeating those same painful lessons even more times! Love yourself for the kindness you extend to others when you're at your best. Love yourself for doing the best you can when you're not at your best. Love yourself for your courage to grow. Love yourself for something beautiful you've created. Love yourself for having the courage to transform.

This step could fill an entire volume of books and, as a Spirit Warrior, is something you will always be refining and reinforcing. Just as our children require and test our unconditional love, so, too, must we do the same for ourselves. Self-love and acceptance and self-esteem are not products for which we strive; these are peaceful states we achieve through our ongoing rituals and new tribal traditions. Seek out books and audio programs on affirmations and self-love. Make loving yourself a part of your new process starting now.

Giving yourself self-love and acceptance is not a one-time box you will be able to check. You will need to repeat your new affirmations of self-acceptance thousands and thousands of times to replace the old beliefs and programming. Begin with I LOVE AND ACCEPT MYSELF JUST AS I AM. Use this affirmation hundreds of times each day to begin the process of realigning yourself with peace and truth.

Ultimately, when you simply love and accept yourself just as you are you will have a spiritual wealth that few ever know.

With the first lesson especially, put this book aside and take some time to begin loving yourself. Take a few days, or a week or more, before going on to the next chapter. There's no hurry to get somewhere else!

Simply practice loving yourself starting now.

How will you do that?

If you don't take the time to start now, then when?

This text can become another TO DO to check and put aside, a short distraction from other concerns, or a real opening into transformation.

Which will you choose?

2

Only you can decide if you are ready to be free.

You are already a powerful force connected here through these words to all that is and all that will ever be. The first lesson tells us that, in order to set yourself free, you love yourself regardless of your life situation. However, only you can decide if you are ready to be free.

While you're deciding if you are ready to be free, one of the most effective tools you can use is the power of forgiveness. Resentment and anger toward yourself and others, no matter how justified such emotions might seem, create darkness within you that eventually becomes a haunting reality. Resentment and anger slowly turn your heart cold and black. If you cannot forgive yourself, you cannot forgive others. And when you cannot forgive others, you block and snuff out your celestial energies. As a Spirit Warrior, you choose to pierce the darkness with the light of forgiveness.

Forgiveness is not about letting people off the hook. Forgiveness does not mean you condone someone else's poor choices and behavior. Forgiveness does not mean you have always made good choices.

The Spirit Warrior travels light.
Forgiveness allows you to put down the burden of the past—the pain, anger and resentment of what is already done—and walk free.

Forgiveness is a sacred gift you give yourself. Imagine the power in allowing yourself to put down the burdens you have carried far too long. Forgiving yourself completely is a great act of self-love. When you, as chief of your own tribe, can grant yourself amnesty for not measuring up to some impossible ideal of perfection, you drive a new stake in the ground that says you are no longer a victim of the past. And when you can forgive yourself, you can extend forgiveness to others. Forgiveness sets you free.

Think of it this way: Not forgiving people, including yourself, drains your energy because justified or not, **you** are the one toiling under the weight of emotion. We sometimes mistakenly believe that our own toxic energy and self-righteousness—*How dare they! I will take this to my grave*—will teach the other person a lesson or give them their due. Whether others get their lessons, however, is not the business of the Spirit Warrior. Most of all, your anger and resentment hurts you. Starting now, as a Spirit Warrior, you choose to use forgiveness to clean the spiritual slate and begin anew.

Spirit Warrior, go within and build a brilliant fire under the night sky.
Listen to the crackle and pop, and breathe in the smoky warmth.
Feel the sacred tribal drumbeat.
Then make your choice: Do you choose being right or letting go?

Being right means you choose to continue dragging around all your old resentments.
Letting go means you choose to unload those heavy emotions into the fire and celebrate
as they burn away into the freedom of nothingness.

Which do you choose?

As a Spirit Warrior, everything in your life starts right now. No longer do you blame others for what you think, believe, feel and do. As a Spirit Warrior, all paths lead back to you. You and only you are the maker of your life. And when you make your inner life, no one can take it away. That is genuine and authentic power. That is your goal as a Spirit Warrior. Forgiveness is an act of genuine and authentic power because it gives you freedom. Forgiveness is a choice you make. Being free is a choice you make. In freeing others to be who they are, you also set yourself free.

The next step is up to you: All you have to do is decide to be free, and you will be free. Of course, the ego voice will probably pipe up immediately: *That's preposterous! It can't be that simple. Don't fall for this nonsense.*

Don't fight the voice for the fight always weakens us. Just let the voice be. And in that space, listen to the growing voice of your highest Self whispering the truth.

I am willing to keep opening the doors in myself
To meet the Ghost,
The essence of what is
And rejoice with knowing.

There's a beautiful place, you will see,
When you put down The Fight
And look and see
You have been here all along.

Peace and stillness are yours.
Beauty and truth spread infinite
And touch the essence at the edges
Of your humanity.

Float on the Ocean of Love,
That infinite nothingness within that you cannot think
In your mind,
But you know in your heart.

I give my hand to Spirit to lead the way
To a greatness
In the infinite space
Within.

Understandably, many people survive severe levels of trauma that would make forgiveness seem unthinkable. Forgiving someone who inflicted abuse on you or another—whether verbal, physical, mental or sexual—may seem counter-productive and even impossible. Not forgiving someone who intentionally hurt you or an innocent child seems completely justified. Anyone who harms the innocent and defenseless tests the limits of our forgiveness, or rather our ability to extend love no matter what.

If you are a victim or witness to abuse, talking to a good therapist will greatly assist you in finding your peace. Ultimately, no matter what others around us did or didn't do, we must find our own peace. Again, forgiveness is not condoning what the other person did. Forgiveness is a tool so that you no longer have to be the emotional pack mule for other people's garbage. Forgiveness is the tool you use to free yourself, not someone else.

Do what feels right for you. In some instances, you may want to send a hand-written note. Or maybe meet for coffee and forgive the person face-to-face. For others a phone call might feel more appropriate. In many cases you will not want to have any physical contact and may choose to write your forgiveness in a journal, say it privately in a prayer or even write a letter that you may or may not send. Other times it may be a deceased person you will need to forgive. You can do so through prayer or meditation or in your dreams. Most importantly, forgive people in whatever way feels right for you. Short and simple, without a lot of explanation or discussion is usually the most powerful.

I forgive myself.
I forgive you.

I will no longer let the past control what I feel in my heart.
I will no longer be the tribal keeper of old anger and resentment.
In this moment, I reclaim my power and set myself free.

We are now both free.

That's it. No need to dredge up and rehash the old incident and who did what to whom or when and why. Release your attachment to being right, let go in a spirit of surrender and trust, and then grant forgiveness. Some people will be easier to forgive than others. Just keep forgiving until you find your peace. When you can think about the person or incident and be peaceful, then you have let it go. When you let go, you create a clear space into which new blessings and experiences will flow.

Spirit Warrior, are you ready to forgive?

If so, then make a list of those you need to forgive. Put yourself first on that list. Write the name of each person and the hurt you experienced.

Then for each, begin your own tribal forgiveness ceremony using the ideas from this chapter or those of your own creation.

Starting now, take a few minutes each day to practice forgiveness and observe how this practice changes the way you feel about yourself and others.

3

Getting ready to be free can take time.

Your entire life can change faster than you can finish reading this sentence. In other words, you could have already made the decision to be free. When you are free, you start doing what you know you need to do.

Did you decide to be free?

Probably not. One of the most difficult steps is the unofficial step that happens before you choose to change: getting-ready-to-be-free. Or getting ready to change. Getting ready to start the new diet on Monday. Getting ready to talk to Mom or Dad. Getting ready to stop smoking. Getting ready to make the phone call to set the appointment that will start the process of getting ready to change.

You become a Spirit Warrior the moment you are truly ready to be free.
This desire for freedom emanates and pulses from your heart space, your soul.
Beware, for your mind (ego) will fear and resist you joining this new tribe of freedom.

You must continually hone your warrior skills to razor precision in order to keep slipping past the mind, undetected, to your soul.

We humans don't like change because all change, or evolution, pushes us out of our comfort zones and creates uncertainty, anxiety and fear. We know instinctively that to evolve we may need to endure uncomfortable feelings. We say we want the change—eat better, work out, forgive others, leave behind unhealthy patterns, stop procrastinating—but we don't want to feel the pain of the unknown. That's why we can spend days, weeks, months, or our whole lives getting ready to change. Sometimes our life is over, and we are still getting ready to change.

It's okay if you're still getting ready to change. You are going to become a Spirit Warrior. Change is not an easy step for this means you must be willing to surrender your old ways.

> *Freedom and beauty are not destinations*
> *But rather smooth fibers in the tapestry of Self.*
> *That freedom is yours for the asking;*
> *You will travel far to walk through this warrior crucible.*

> *Eventually, you must be willing to kneel at the altar*
> *of your true shining spirit,*
> *palms upturned, and say,*
> *"I am ready to come home to you.*
> *I am ready to be free."*

Being free is not easy. Being free can be terrifying because you leave behind old ways. You may have to leave behind people you love—friends, family members, even spouses and boyfriends and girlfriends—who are not ready to be free. Being free requires tremendous courage on your part because you will let go of what's comfortable and step into what's possible.

And this step comes with a price: great uncertainty. It is a price worth paying. Uncertainty is simply an indicator, a beacon that leads you out of darkness to your spiritual growth and warrior transformation. Do not be hard on yourself if you are still deciding if you are ready to be free. You are not alone if you feel stuck, if you still reach for things to numb the pain and escape the confusion rather than being free. Be gentle with yourself. You are not a bad person; you are a human being like everyone else.

Part of walking the conscious path is being able to tolerate the pain that will set you free. That is the crucible through which every Spirit Warrior walks. You will eventually come to know that emotional pain will not destroy you. You will come to understand, in fact, that pain cannot touch who you truly are. Pain becomes your liberator when you begin to allow it to just be. Avoidance is normal human behavior because we are each genetically hard-wired to seek pleasure and avoid pain. It's the same basic survival instinct that keeps us from touching the hot stove a second time. Therefore, we unconsciously put every choice on a pain-pleasure scale and instinctively follow the path of least pain. We often stay stuck in pain to avoid what we perceive as even greater pain. It's understandable, then, that we would choose to stay, for example, in an emotionally-unhealthy relationship because the imagined hurt of the break-up and the painful aftermath are even worse than the current level of pain. There is another way.

The Spirit Warrior becomes rooted in Mother Earth, leans into the truth and braces for the pain that may come with that truth.

You are already a strong person. And yet you have probably tried many times to use all your strength and willpower to change. You tell yourself, *This time will be different. This time I'm serious.* And you are, no doubt, serious, committed and capable. But yet you do not change, and you still feel lost. The storm clouds of pain do not part. The cold rain of fear and loneliness continue to fall. And eventually the pain leads you back to the very behavior you're trying to change.

• *The pain of not sticking to your healthy eating plan leads you back to overeating.*

• *The pain of a bad break-up leads you to another unhealthy relationship.*

• *The pain of the hangover and morning-after haze leads you back to the drink or drug.*

• *The pain of not taking action leads you to more lost days of procrastinating.*

This is all normal human behavior, which is not to say it is healthy or reflects self-love and acceptance. On a larger scale, witness the cycle of war and violence as normal human behavior that only creates more pain and misery, never lasting peace. And yet, both globally and individually, we stay stuck and resistant to change because we fear the wall of pain we know we must face. This force of resistance is so powerful, Spirit Warrior, that you will run barefoot through fire to avoid your pain. Attempting to physically flee one's internal pain, in fact, is quite common: moving to a new city or state or country to make a new start, endlessly traveling to 'find ourselves', or always changing jobs, houses, and partners.

The answer is never out there. The answer is in you. Instead of running, focus your awareness and observe yourself for thoughts that might indicate resistance to change:

• *Just one more time for a little relief.*

• *Tomorrow will be different.*

• *I'll start next week. I've got too much going on right now.*

• *What's the big deal? I'm not that bad compared to a lot of people.*

• *Everyone's doing it; why should I miss out?*

• *Why be so uptight? If it feels good, do it.*

Don't punish yourself if you uncover this type of thinking. You are not weak or inferior. You are simply protecting yourself from the pain you suspect awaits you when you do what you know you must.

> *The magic of change happens in a single flash of time.*
> *Getting ready to change, however, can take an entire lifetime.*

> *If you haven't changed old patterns, you are still getting ready to change.*

The change that happens in an instant is when you say, "No more. I will not live like this one more day, one more hour or one more minute. I must change now." That's the moment of power when you make a new choice. You shed the old victim skin and become a creator. That's the moment you make the call to find a therapist, or go on-line to look up a support group, or toss out the potato chips and make the call to join a gym. It's the moment when you stand up for yourself in your relationship and speak the truth in your heart. You know the feeling of those moments when you tap your own power, those times when fear and doubt vanish as you summon your inner strength to change and create. You may have forgotten, but you will remember.

> *I am a Spirit Warrior connected to the infinite timetable.*
> *I let go of trying to control how and when the gods will grant me what is right.*
> *I turn my palms upward and simply surrender and trust Spirit.*

As a Spirit Warrior all things begin with you. In every moment, you alone stand between staying stuck in old ways and choosing to use your power to create. Every moment of every day gives you this choice, and you alone are doing the choosing. The thoughts you choose will create your emotions. And your emotions will dictate your actions. Thought—emotion—action. It may sound trivial, but the thoughts you indulge in this moment literally will shape your destiny. You cannot control all the thoughts that pop into your mind, but you can choose the ones to which you'll give permanent space.

You are the shaman of your own soul.
How carefully have you kept watch over your sacred heart space?

You may have allowed all sorts of infiltrators from other tribes to move in and take up permanent residence! The self-defeating beliefs. The negative naysayers. The voices of endless anxiety and worry. Do you allow fear and doubt and unworthiness to run rampant? We all do at times. Without judging yourself, it's time to clear out your sacred temples and inner emotional sanctuaries. Adopt the knowing that you can change starting in this moment. You can kick beliefs out of your head without any advance notice.

Make a list, Spirit Warrior, of the disempowering beliefs you need to clear out.
Any belief that will not bring you peace is no longer welcome in your
sacred heart space.

Once you've singled out the problem tribal members, the ones who have been tearing
down the walls of your self-esteem and riddling your truth and clarity with negativity,
banish them from the tribe.

That's right: Tell them to get out and send them into the wilderness now.

Do you feel resistance about serving notice to your faulty beliefs? Feel that resistance and go ahead anyway. When you move through resistance, you weaken resistance. Fear and resistance begin to die when you acknowledge them—*Okay, I see you there Fear and Resistance*—and instead of running, you simply move through them. In this spiritual journey, fear and resistance have no countermove when you begin doing the things you fear, when you no longer identify with resistance but use it as fire for action. Do the things you fear now. Follow the trail of your resistance rather than believing it. Let your pain and resistance be indicators for what you need to do. Take action now, Spirit Warrior, for now is your moment of power.

Look inside, Spirit Warrior, and ask yourself this powerful question:
How long are you going to take to get ready to change?

That's the Big Question that awaits you.

Do you need ten seconds? Five more minutes? How about until tonight? Is one more day enough? A week? Eight months? Two years? Ten years? Your entire lifetime? Ten lifetimes? You alone decide.

It really does not matter; the lessons you need to learn and the changes you need to make are infinitely patient. The lessons will wait until you are ready. The lessons will wait a hundred lifetimes. And when you are ready to change, in that moment of decision, you will marshal the entire power of the Universe to assist you on your path.

If you are willing to listen, you already know the answers to all your questions. Do not look outside yourself, Spirit Warrior, for the answers are there inside you. No one else can tell you the answers to your own questions. Nor do you need anyone else to give you permission to find your own answers and set yourself free. The difficulty and the beauty of the spiritual path are inseparable, for when you clear the clouds of confusion and doubt, all that remains is your own brilliant clarity. Step into that clarity, right now, and you are free. You alone get to make that choice: step through and gain passage to a new and better life or remain on the other side where fear keeps you waiting. And waiting. And waiting.

Are you still getting ready to be free?
Or are you ready to be free now?

If you can truthfully answer YES, then put this book aside and spend a few days celebrating your commitment to change (this is a powerful way to love and affirm yourself).

If your answer is NO, then put this book aside and spend a few days exploring what needs to happen for you to be ready. Write your answers in your journal and share them with your support guides.

4

You can choose true freedom and genuine peace.

This is a truth you know deep in your heart—that the power to be free is already yours—but it is a truth you may have forgotten. When you know and embrace this truth, then you are free and your training is complete. It takes some time for most of us, however, to discover, understand and embrace this truth. And then even when we set ourselves free, we sometimes forget and have to do some more training as a reminder. True freedom and genuine peace, then, become an ongoing, moment-by-moment process. You always have the option of choosing that which contradicts your truth and, therefore, will not serve you long term. No person, place or thing outside yourself gives you freedom and peace; the Spirit Warrior creates freedom and peace within through the power of choice.

That is what becoming a Spirit Warrior is all about: awareness. Discovering and living your own inner truth. And then doing the things you need to do so you never forget. That is the elusive secret for which you have been searching; that is the knowledge that sets you free; that is the key to all your freedoms: spiritual, emotional, mental, and physical. Even your financial freedom. Yes, all the freedom you ever wanted is not out there, it's right there, in your heart, waiting for you.

Only you can choose to open the door.
Will you open the door?

You do not need to learn anything new to become free. You do not need to read this book or any other or seek a wise sage on a high mountain in Tibet. You do not need to go through twelve steps or five years of therapy or give yourself disempowering labels to become free. You do not need to recite Hail Marys, go to Mecca or sit in meditation until you get leg cramps. You do not need to shave your head or find your soul mate to become free. The answer to what you seek is not in another audio program or self-help book or at your church.

All you need to do to be free is remember who you have always been—
You are infinity, an unborn and undying soul of energy.

Good therapy and support programs and church and all your other tools are helpful guides on your journey, but the part we often forget is that every answer to every question is not out there.

The answer is in Spirit, which is in you.
Nothing is missing;
Learning is simply remembering.

Young children, especially around age three, are our best reminder for what it is like to be free and at peace. If you have children of your own, you understand this truth. If you don't have children of your own, borrow someone else's. Make playing with children an ongoing part of your Spirit Warrior training. Playing with children is the most direct route to teaching adults how to be free again.

A healthy three-year-old child instinctively follows all the lessons contained in all the world's spiritual teachings. Children love themselves unconditionally because they have not yet learned to be critical and judge themselves harshly. Children are free because they don't dwell in the past or gaze into the future; children live in the here-and-now. Children do not yet have any unhealthy patterns to untangle, a host of mental fears, or any problem staying in the flow of life. Before adults have time to condition these young people, children live the concepts of spirituality and truth without any intellectual understanding of these concepts. They walk the talk without any intellectual grasp of the talk.

Spirit Warrior, choose now to become the young, happy child that you are and
ground yourself in joy, peace and love.
Make the choice to release fear, resentment, guilt, shame, regret and anger.

Step outside and look at the sky and just observe your breath for a few minutes.
Let go of thinking. When you feel grounded in your breath, thank the clouds and stars
for giving you strength.

Are you ready to set yourself free now?
Or do you need more time to get ready?

Take a few days to record your discoveries in your journal or to not journal at all and just be.

5

Understand your patterns.

What patterns do you use to soothe yourself?

Do you eat to feel comfort? Do you pick up cigarettes or alcohol to erase that void inside? Do you stay in relationships that aren't working? Do you smoke pot or drink wine to escape? Do you use your work as a pattern to escape yourself? Do you look at pornography or have sex with people you don't really know to medicate the loneliness?

Every human being develops and uses patterns of behavior. Some patterns serve us well: brush and floss, send thank-you notes, get regular exercise, eat your vegetables. Other patterns hinder and limit us. We numb out to avoid the pain of facing ourselves. And through lifelong conditioning, we learn to cling to the patterns we've developed even when those patterns stifle us. Our patterns can devolve into compulsions and addictions, which are just habits with more severe consequences. Instead of unravelling and healing our own pain, we often grasp outside ourselves—new relationship, a better house, more money, another college degree, more sex in better positions—because that is our conditioned pattern. Except the patterns don't work, and the lasting peace we seek slips through our fingers like sand. Still, we become slave to these same patterns in a desperate attempt to shake the dull fog and pain. Herein is your mission, Spirit Warrior: To free yourself of your old conditioning and patterns.

Pausing at still waters and simply looking at the reality of your reflection can be terrifying.

Most of us run for a long time before we're willing to stop and really look at our own patterns.

You become a Spirit Warrior the moment you stop running.

Many distractions are not as compulsive or as obvious as full-blown addictions. Watching too much TV may not ruin your life, but it can still be a debilitating pattern if it holds you back. These behaviors can be particularly difficult to see as problem patterns because there may never be a cataclysmic event or dramatic moment-of-truth to shake us from our deep slumber.

For example, do you use reading as a way to check out and disconnect from yourself? Do you spend most nights flipping through TV channels or playing video games? Do you stay in a job that gives you little sense of passion or purpose? Do you socialize with people who don't really support you simply because you don't know how to say NO? Do you go shopping and buy things because you don't want to talk to your husband or wife about the real issues?

The Spirit Warrior knows and accepts the truth that whether young, old, rich, poor, idyllic childhood or not, we all have healthy and unhealthy patterns. You may not remember what true freedom feels like, but you know what true freedom is not: living far below your true potential. Behaving in ways that bring you and those around you pain is a roadblock to fulfilling your potential.

Patterns of distraction can become seductive alternatives to facing one's truth and creating true freedom.

Spirit Warrior, what are your patterns?

Do your patterns serve you or bind you?

Here's a hint: Take a look at the things you defend the most. We often minimize what we fear giving up:

• *I'm not that bad.*

• *A few drinks to take off the edge is no big deal.*

• *I can stop whenever I want.*

• *Yeah, I work too many hours, but you can't succeed in my business if you don't put in the time.*

What we call our unhealthy patterns—bad habits, compulsions, addictions—isn't that important. Instead, look beyond the labels to the truth and don't feel obligated to label yourself in any way that doesn't feel right to you. And don't worry about comparing your patterns with other people's patterns. Thinking we can change other people's patterns, actually, is an unhealthy pattern in itself. If you've tried to change someone, you will probably encounter the lessons of acceptance, surrender and humility. The Spirit Warrior is powerful, but no one has the power to change others. The Spirit Warrior keeps the focus only on what you have the power to change: YOU. Other people must do the same for themselves.

> *Patterns become unhealthy when thoughts and behaviors are a solution*
> *for life's problems,*
> *for your anxiety,*
> *for your fear,*
> *for your pain,*
>
> *Because then you are not free.*

Being twenty-five pounds overweight may not ever destroy your life, but you sense that nagging lack of freedom. *Why do I keep eating until I'm numb and bloated if it's not how I want to feel?*

Another way many of us cope is to act out fears and emotions sexually. And yet, having anonymous one-night stands because we feel empty and lonely will not bring true connection and intimacy. And yet the ego voice will defend your behaviors by declaring your freedom and independence to make your own choices.

A good indicator is to observe how you feel after any behavior. If you feel empty after doing something, you are trying to erase your loneliness and pain through that behavior. The exercise here is not to judge yourself, but to accept the reality of the patterns you must change to be free. You can begin affirming what you've already learned in your Spirit Warrior training:

> *1. I love and accept myself.*
> *2. I forgive myself for the past.*
> *3. I choose true freedom and genuine peace.*
> *4. I am willing to change.*

As a Spirit Warrior, you own your whole Self. You embrace all your strengths and the areas where you are weak. Embracing weakness is key in tapping into your infinite power. No one is without weakness, yet most of us try to cover up and run from our inadequacies. We project a mask of invulnerability and strength, but inside we feel small and afraid. As a Spirit Warrior, you open your eyes and accept it all. In doing so, you begin living from strength without letting your unchallenged patterns control your behavior. Understanding those patterns is a huge step toward your freedom.

Begin now to look into the still waters of your true Self.
Simply become willing to see.

What patterns do you use to soothe yourself?

To break through old denial and patterns of avoidance, take the time to honestly reflect on the above question. Then write your answers on paper, speak your truth aloud and then, ideally, share your discovery with a trusted friend, therapist or loved one.

6

Connect with others who are getting ready to be free.

(Just don't tie yourself to the bridge once you cross.)

Spirit Warrior, you are remembering a profound truth: True freedom and genuine peace are yours right now if that is what you choose. Not tomorrow or next week, but right now. However, because most of us need at least some emotional healing, making the jump from where we start to true freedom is usually a longer process. Yes, at the moment of decision, you are free in that instant. Your life changes in a flash of time so quick it could happen before you finish reading this sentence.

Did you just set yourself free?

If so, put down this book because your journey is complete. You are already home. Give this book to someone else who is getting ready to be free. If you did not set yourself free, that is perfectly acceptable, too. You are still getting ready.

Until you reach that moment of decision, connecting with others who are also getting ready to be free—and those who are free—will greatly accelerate your Spirit Warrior training. The Spirit Warrior asks others for help and therein begins a new life of strength through acceptance, surrender and trust. Sharing your struggles to change with other people who are committed to changing is a very powerful experience.

A good connecting place for an apprentice Spirit Warrior is a support group of like-minded people who are committed to changing. Twelve-step groups, for example, are the most well-known and are now available for virtually any type of pattern you're trying to change. What began as casual gatherings of alcoholics in the 1940s now includes meetings for drugs, sex, food, smoking, gambling, compulsive spending, relationships and more. Meetings are regular and free.

There's nothing magical or mystical about the twelve steps. The twelve steps are yet another tool to help you find your freedom. Although the Spirit Warrior does not mistake the map for the territory, the twelve steps do provide an excellent framework for leading us through the process of acceptance, surrender and trust. The steps also show us how to look at and embrace our strengths and weaknesses, find our own spirituality and clean up mistakes from when we were less conscious. The steps lead us full circle by giving to others the peace and joy you find.

Again, the greatest value in the steps is that they get you moving (emotionally) and doing your work. And doing your own work, whether through twelve steps or some other method, is the responsibility every Spirit Warrior embraces.

As you move closer to freedom, Spirit Warrior, be vigilant to not substitute the support group for the truth itself. There is no freedom in turning the twelve steps, or any other program of support or therapy, into a new religion and structure that binds you in a victim mindset. Instead, set yourself free by using your support as a bridge to reach safety and then continuing on your journey to freedom. Being free does not resign you to a life of having conquered your old patterns, but still replaying the graphic details and horror and never quite shaking that Big Lie that you are still inferior, unworthy and not good enough.

However, this does not mean that once you break the old patterns you will dump the support people who helped you get better. You don't need to walk the Earth as a silent and independent sage to demonstrate your freedom. Your freedom is humility and balance, and the Spirit Warrior finds humility and balance by staying connected to all that is, including those who love and support you, *and* walking your own path without feeling obligated to label yourself, be a victim or keep rehashing that old story that no longer controls you unless you let it. Some may call this denial, but denial is what keeps people stuck. A self-responsibility that is interdependent, rather than dependent, is not denial.

You can leave behind unhealthy patterns for good. The Zen term for instant awakening is *satori*. The experience is like stepping through a gate that perhaps took many years of struggle to find. Then, in literally a moment, you walk through the gate to the other side. What you find behind that gate is the peace and freedom and stillness for which you searched so hard for so many years. This process happens not through willpower or determination or trying to conquer old ways, but rather by simply surrendering and being willing to allow a new way of being.

That which you seek you cannot find.
You must simply be willing.
Let go and allow your freedom to happen.

This path is about finding your freedom and that includes the freedom to not take on a new victim identity regardless of what anyone tells you. Introducing yourself with labels and faults and reliving old wounds and endlessly retelling your dramatic story to supportive people can become a seductive path. There is a fine line between healthy acknowledgement of one's issues and a commitment to live a better life and believing the old voice that still says you're not good enough and never will be. Who you truly are is so much more than any label you give yourself.

The Spirit Warrior learns to walk the delicate line between that old demon of denial and the bliss of freedom.

True bliss makes no apologies for shedding the old victim skin once and for all.

Stepping into the fierce flow of your highest spirit energy can be quite terrifying. Many choose to instead stay in the comfort zone where things are much better than before, but not so good as to challenge their concepts of deservability and highest potential.

Yes, Spirit Warrior, use all the tools and support to get yourself safely to the other side. And then have the courage, once you cross the bridge, to continue finding deeper and more expansive levels of freedom. The bridge often saves our life by carrying us across great peril, so it's normal to get attached to the bridge. But trying to bring the bridge along once you're safely across the chasm only keeps you stuck. You'll be hanging around the bridge as even greater joys await you on your path. Being on the safe side of the bridge is an infinitely better place to be than before, but being sober and stuck is still not true freedom. The Spirit Warrior learns to travel light and not take on new dogmas or human-made hierarchies that insert themselves between you and your freedom, between you and your highest Self, between you and the eternal spirit.

If you think of your freedom as connecting to your inner spirit—what twelve-step programs call a *higher power*, what religions call God, Allah and Buddha, what yogis call *prana*, that cosmic energy that binds us all—then anything that comes between you and that inner flow of wisdom is a filter clouding your freedom. Here are some powerful Spirit Warrior tactics:

Drop the labels: Learn who you are and what self-destructive patterns you have used to soothe yourself and commit to changing those patterns. Then stop choosing self-defeating labels. The labels we give ourselves are often loaded with judgments. Do not feel compelled to explain or defend yourself when well-meaning people tell you that dropping your labels means you are back on a dangerous and slippery slope of denial that will lead you straight back to the old ways. Do what feels right, and remember that you only have to answer to your highest Self. Literally, this is between you and your God. You cannot be in denial if what you are doing brings you true inner peace. And by demonstrating an even higher level of freedom, you become a role model to your support friends. You are no longer a victim; you are a creator.

Drop the story: Understand your history and how you came to the moment that is now. Embrace all aspects of your story as perfect and necessary lessons on your journey. Resolve all the old emotional wounds, hurts and anger. Keep forgiving yourself and others. Then choose the life you want to create and drop the old story. Just choose to leave it behind because it is dead, an empty shell of what used to be. What happened in the past no longer dictates what you will do today. You might get sympathy and nods of approval when you keep re-telling the old story, but you stay rooted in the past rather than creating what you want now. Instead, tell the new story about who you are and what you are creating with your newfound freedom. You are no longer a victim; you are a creator.

Drop the victim: When you choose to be free, it's like stopping alongside the road and dropping off the old victim. As much pain as that part of you caused, it also helped get you through the tough times. Say good-bye to the part of you that kept you afraid and blamed other people and events for your unhappiness or problems or lack of success. You no longer need that part of you because you are no longer stuck. You are now responsible for everything that comes into your life. You are no longer a victim; you are a creator.

As a Spirit Warrior, you are taking responsibility for yourself and your happiness by seeking out new connections. A good therapist or other spiritual guide can help you understand your own patterns. One of the best things about spiritual guides is the ability to affirm and reflect back to you the shining parts of yourself as well as the areas you need to improve, and to do so without judgment. Your guides will help you see and speak your own truth. You can also connect to guides through self-help books and audio programs. Classes and workshops in journaling, dream analysis, yoga, meditation, music and other spiritual pursuits are great ways to connect with others in new ways. You can even start your own support group of like-minded cosmic travelers. You can even start a Spirit Warrior study group.

The Spirit Warrior embraces the strength of surrender by asking for help. Asking for help and support accelerates your growth and evolution. No truly successful person walks the path alone. Asking for help is a cause set in motion. Your decision to be free will in turn elicit the support and guidance you need. And then something magical happens. As you get healthier and healthier, you become the source of support and guidance to people joining you on the path. In a twelve-step program, that is the final step: *Having had a spiritual awakening, we tried to carry this message to others.*

Like a young warrior, you are beginning the journey through your own undiscovered, personal landscape. You are strong and focused and disciplined in your training and preparation. You will have to take every single step yourself and marshal your powerful will to overcome the pain and fatigue and biting cold. Yet, you increase your chances of success when you bring along a strong team of support people, fellow travelers and wilderness guides. You need people at your side who have been there before and know the terrain and danger spots. You will walk up and down each mountain, but you will need the help and support of others to do so.

Right now, there is a team of professionals, new friends, and emotional guides awaiting your decision to begin your expedition. They are prepared to help you read the stars of your own inner clues. They will teach you how to survive in the wilderness. They will help you build your own brilliant bonfire of freedom. They will nudge you back on course when you stray from the path. They will beat the celebration drums when you reach every summit.

You will be amazed at the resources and support and love you tap into once you simply continue the journey. You may even be at the very beginning, which is making that first call for help. When you pick up the phone or go to your first meeting or tell a friend you need to get some help, you have begun a voyage that is more powerful than you could ever imagine.

In that moment when you surrender and ask for help,
you are responding to a spiritual beacon deep within yourself.

Your spirit is not of this Earth.
Your spirit is calling you home to yourself.

Always do what feels right in your heart. What works for you will be different than what works for her. What works for her will be different than what works for him. When and how all this happens is different for everyone. Ultimately, what works for you and brings *you* true peace is always the right path.

YOUR COSMIC JOURNEY—

This concludes Part One of your Spirit Warrior training. The real power is in applying what you learn and using your new knowledge to condition yourself in more empowering ways. Here is your test question:

The Big Question:
Are you ready to be free, or are you still getting ready to be free?

The Spirit Warrior knows that you don't so much find freedom as you become freedom. Therefore, you adopt a disciplined practice of reconditioning and realigning your energies. Discipline is not to be avoided because it's uncomfortable. *Uncomfortable* is just the feeling of old comfort zones expanding. Therefore, the Spirit Warrior learns to love discipline. Discipline equals freedom, and freedom is the goal.

Below are the first six lessons each distilled into a single affirmation. These six core beliefs are the new mental tapes the Spirit Warrior runs not once or twice or a hundred times, but thousands and thousands of times, day after day, week after week, month after month. This is the same repetitive conditioning system that constructed the mental patterns you have today. Use this knowledge to return to the pure state of your original mind.

1. I love and accept myself, and I am free.
2. I forgive myself and all others, and I am free.
3. I choose to create miracles right now, and I am free.
4. I choose peace, and I am free.
5. I release all old patterns, and I am free.
6. I surrender and ask for help, and I am free.

Just be willing, and if you aren't ready to choose willingness, step outside and look at the sky. Just be silent and let willingness find you. If you listen, the stars will lead you to new possibilities. Love yourself as you would a newborn member of the tribe for that is who you are.

Points to Ponder

• Do you choose to cling to those same old affirmations, thoughts, beliefs and patterns that bring pain?

• Do you choose to keep acting out the same patterns, or are you ready to be free?

• Are you willing to believe?

• Are you willing to surrender?

• Are you willing to try something new?

PART II

Your sacred quest

1

Surrender to your truth.

As a Spirit Warrior, truth is your mission. You will dig deep and uncover a rare and ancient gem: your own true, shining Self. The Spirit Warrior knows nothing gets better until you reveal and embrace the truth. Finding and speaking your own truth is another gift you give yourself. But this gem is usually not on the surface where you might accidentally trip over it. You earn this gift through self discovery.

As a Spirit Warrior, you know the power of surrounding yourself with supportive guides, therapists and clergy to lead the way—friends to cheer you on—but ultimately only you have the knowledge to find your own answers.

When we do not speak our truth, we choose fear over freedom.

What truth is deep in your heart that you have not spoken?

The tribe of Spirit Warriors embraces self honesty as a powerful tool. Like a sharp blade, being honest with yourself cuts through the thick overgrowth of denial, excuses and distraction to a clearing that holds the unchanging core of your truth.

Your journey does not come with a precise point-to-point map with GPS coordinates. The map will be revealed only after you've stepped into the unknown. Simply begin with the mission of finding truth and acceptance knowing that the journey will be fraught with uncertainty, fear, painful emotional battles, and much change. Ultimately, the only way to pick up the trail of your truth is to enter the jungle, the undiscovered territory within yourself, and begin searching. Even as the stifling heat drains your energy and branches sting your face, you march forward. Straight into the darkness and fear is the only way to freedom, and you earn this freedom through the sweat and toil of each step.

Willingness and surrender are like giant
Alarm chimes that signal
The Gods
To open the door to Self.

The Spirit Warrior commits fully to the path knowing that the path, the journey, will eventually bring you home to yourself. That is, if you are willing to continue no matter how difficult the path becomes, no matter how fierce the heat of honesty sears your preconceptions and burns away your illusions and old patterns.

The Spirit Warrior follows the trail that is being revealed. Just follow. No effort. No strain. No force. Believe. Trust. Be. You are near. Very near to the treasure.

When we are ready, truly ready,
The truth will be given to us.
Not a false truth from our mind
But a deep knowing from our heart
That lay hidden like secret treasure.

Do not be surprised when you lift the lid
To find something staring back you do not recognize.
Simply know that the truth is real,
And what you see here
Is all you will ever need.

The journey of facing the truth is often very painful. The Spirit Warrior does not run from pain. Yes, the truth shall set you free; however, the truth may also bring you deep pain. Avoidance keeps the pain away on one level and on a different level creates the pain of not living your truth. So while avoidance insulates you somewhat from pain, it's not very effective and never works long-term. The Spirit Warrior knows that the pain of a wasted or misguided life is far worse than anything you will have to endure to be free. And in that moment of clarity you set off on the trail.

When you find the treasure—your own truth—you will know.
How will you know? You will just know.

Trust that feeling inside you've already experienced in other ways.
How do you know your favorite color? You just know.

Most importantly, be willing to embrace your truth even if you do not understand it yet.
You will.
Trust.

Spirit could not deceive you.

• When your truth tells you you're going to need help to stop the patterns or behaviors you've been using, then you seek that help.

• When your truth tells you your relationship is not working anymore, then you owe it to yourself to speak that truth.

• When your truth says you are in the wrong career, then you owe it to yourself to look into the career you really want.

• When your truth tells you that what you're doing, or not doing, isn't working, then you owe it to yourself to speak that truth.

Finding your truth, once you are ready to listen, may not be that difficult. You probably already know your truth, but have just allowed yourself to push it away. Once you accept and speak your own truth, the difficult part is walking through the door of change. Speaking your truth may disappoint people you love. Speaking your truth may cause you immediate pain. Speaking your truth may cause change and upheaval in your life. Speaking your truth, in short, may make your life appear worse than before.

In the film *The Lord of the Rings*, the reluctant warrior Frodo Baggins is forced into facing his truth when he says, "I wish the Ring had never come to me. I wish none of this had happened."

Gandalf, the ancient and wise wizard, replies, "So do all who live to see such times, but that is not for them to decide. All we have to decide is what to do with the time that is given to us."

What will you decide to do, Spirit Warrior, with your time? What is your truth? This is where you earn your mettle as a Spirit Warrior. Now rather than running, you will use the emotions that come up—whether anger, fear, shame, guilt, anxiety or panic—as fuel for your growth. Pain, when you follow its cues, becomes a compass. Pain tells you what's working and what's not working in your life. Pain becomes another valuable friend and guide. And like Frodo, you may also begin your voyage reluctantly. This is perfectly okay. Begin anyway.

As a Spirit Warrior, you honor yourself by asking better questions to uncover your own truths. Spend some time writing, or talking about, your answers to these questions:

• What's my truth in this moment?

• What am I feeling?

• What am I trying to medicate or cover up with my behavior?

• What truth am I covering up with my old patterns and avoidances?

• From what am I trying to hide?

• What do I want my life to mean?

• What truth do I need to speak that I am holding back because I do not want to disappoint another?

The Big Question:
Are you ready to be free?
Or are you still getting ready to be free?

As a Spirit Warrior, you always stand between two worlds. One is that of the lesser Self, that part of you who is unconscious and irresponsible. This path feels easier. This is the path where the old ways, the old beliefs and old comforts soothe and deceive you with distraction and myth. This illusion might work in the short-term, but never over time. Getting drunk tonight may block out the fear, but the truth is patient and always bubbles back up. Eating to feel comforted works today, but when you later feel sick, the truth will be there waiting.

The other world that awaits is that of your truth, your highest, conscious and responsible Self. This path is more difficult because it shatters illusion and leads to true freedom. The decision is yours alone.

What are you waiting for?
Speak, or write your truth(s), and see what happens.

2

Become a renegade warrior.

As a Spirit Warrior, you get to become a renegade. Not in the outward sense, but a renegade within your own mind. You wrap your soul in tribal robes, ride up on a stallion and pierce the old mental authority with a sharpened spear. You conduct raids and begin disrupting the old rules, beliefs and self-talk. You set fire to the old doubts, fears and conditioning. You kneel in prayer at sunset and celebrate your new renegade ways.

Be vigilant for your mind will not like that you are challenging it, and
your mind will rise up and fight back.

Like an old chant you no longer want to sing,
the mind can only play the notes it sees.

Are you ready to script your own new triumphant themes?

Be a renegade with a purpose—The Spirit Warrior rebels against unchallenged ideas about your life and your purpose. Put on the cloak of your purpose and wear it proudly. As a Spirit Warrior, you are free to pursue what brings you joy and fulfillment. The important distinction is why you pursue whatever you choose. In becoming a Spirit Warrior, you are no longer bound by the cultural standard that says you must accomplish X-Y-Z to be worthy. To be acceptable. To arrive.

As a Spirit Warrior, you know the truth. Nothing you accomplish, do, or achieve on this planet is going to finally make you okay. You are already perfect and complete. With this inner truth, a Spirit Warrior pursues the highest vision simply for the joy and fun and challenge and excitement the process brings. This process becomes your purpose and, ultimately, your prosperity. The soul's transformation is your reward, not the illusion of a payoff at the end of the journey.

Hidden within your spirit is your calling. And your calling is your highest Self and purpose. You've stopped the denial, the running, and uncovered your truth. Now ask your heart what you want your life to be. And more importantly, why you want what you want.

Uncover your beautiful and sacred purpose because this is your one life to be the person you were meant to be.

Perhaps you always wanted to go to college. Or maybe you started and never finished. You know in your heart this is what you always wanted. As a Spirit Warrior, you will follow this path simply because this is what excites you and your spirit. Not because a college degree will validate you or make you worthy or worthwhile. Your worth is intact just by being you. Maybe you want to paint. Or learn to scuba dive. Or work with kids. Or volunteer at a hospital. Or heal your relationship with Mom and Dad.

As a Spirit Warrior, you challenge your thinking with tough questions:

• *How long am I going to run around like a scared little boy or a scared little girl?*

• *What price will I pay if I continue doing what I'm doing (or not doing)?*

• *Is what I'm about to do going to bring me peace?*

• *What joy will I create if I allow myself to succeed?*

The Spirit Warrior knows you best serve the world by following your own unique path and sharing your gifts. Release any old guilt because the Universe rejoices most when you are happy, free and doing what you love. Here are three more questions to point the way to your purpose:

How may I best serve in this lifetime?

What is it I need to know?

When do I feel my absolute best?

As a Spirit Warrior, you practice discipline. Once you know what you want and why you want it, discipline becomes a valuable tool of the renegade. Like a heavy boulder pushed downhill, discipline clears a path through the spiritual enemies of avoidance, distraction and procrastination (which are all just different masks for fear). You know in your heart what must be done. You are no longer afraid; you are strong. You develop discipline through routines and rituals that may not always be pleasant: expressing your emotions, confronting your spouse, getting to the gym before work, passing on dessert, getting up early each morning to meditate and spending time with yourself. Doing your work. Transforming your Self.

Most people see discipline as painful bondage.

The Spirit Warrior embraces discipline because discipline brings freedom.

You are unlearning many old ways of thinking and behaving; discipline is a powerful tool to establish your new patterns. Discipline provides structure and a framework around which new modes of operating take shape. The Spirit Warrior doesn't necessarily like discipline any more than other people, but the Spirit Warrior knows and loves the effect discipline creates.

Are you willing to allow yourself to succeed now?
Or are you still getting ready?

Either way, what small, new disciplines and routines can you start today that will bring you the freedom you deserve?

As a reminder, are you finding ways to love and affirm yourself every day?
Are you taking a few minutes to forgive yourself and others each day, or are you choosing to carry around toxic emotions?
Are you speaking and living your truth?

Most importantly, are you taking responsibility for your own transformation, or are you passively reading and hoping something outside yourself will magically change your life?

3

Make friends with uncertainty and embrace being alone.

Paradoxically, when you create true freedom you will also have much uncertainty. Freedom brings change. Change brings the stress and challenge of living in the unknown. As you succeed in changing old ways, therefore, uncertainty will be your constant companion. As a Spirit Warrior, you make friends with uncertainty.

As a Spirit Warrior, you are on a lifelong mission to be your own emotional keeper. Staying on the path is the focus for there is no end destination. When you are on the path you have already arrived. And on the path you will continue to uncover and discover new parts of yourself. Uncertainty is a good sign that you are moving forward. Uncertainty comes in many forms including anxiety and fear even to the Spirit Warrior who has broken free. As a Spirit Warrior you will not live a life without challenges, stress and anxiety. You will be, however, better equipped to handle these challenges and other emotions when they arise. The spiritual life does not grant you all the answers to all the questions; the spiritual life shows you how to find peace while living in the questions.

Once you set yourself free, along with much uncertainty, you will often be alone. The Spirit Warrior knows to be alone is different from being lonely. Being lonely is when you are disconnected from yourself regardless of how many people are around you. As a Spirit Warrior you know that no one is going to save you emotionally. We are each responsible for saving ourselves.

Again, the paradox is that as you find your spiritual freedom, you will see you are, in fact, never truly alone. The Spirit Warrior finds this freedom within by connecting to the nameless cosmic source. You will not need anyone or anything outside yourself to validate the inner peace and connection you feel. For the Spirit Warrior, this is where true intimacy begins: with Self. Your alone time is no longer something to be feared; being alone is the tablet upon which you carve deep new understandings about who you are and your purpose on this planet. Channelling your focus and energy to making your relationship with yourself the best it can be improves your life and all your other relationships. Why? Your relationships work better because you are not interested in changing others—only in changing yourself. And when you learn and grow and expand, the entire world benefits.

One of the unexpected outcomes of true freedom is that you step out from the pack. You may have to leave behind people you love and about whom you care deeply. Setting yourself free means you are responsible for healing your own pain and no one else's. This approach protects the Spirit Warrior from getting entangled or lost in other people's pain. You now redirect your energies to your pursuits. You choose not to worry about trying to fix or make other people happy. You keep your focus on you while being empathetic and loving toward others. This can be a difficult balance to find.

You will probably have to set new boundaries with loved ones, friends, co-workers, spouses, boyfriends and girlfriends. When you set boundaries, you must brace yourself because the reaction from others will often be strong. A Spirit Warrior on the path is threatening to those who are still stuck. People will sense your growth is moving you in new directions, which means, perhaps, pulling you away from friends and loved ones. Out of their own fears, they may lash out and label your new ways and behaviors weird. They may long for the good 'ole days and the old you. They react not because they want to hurt you, but because they do not want to lose you. The old you is comforting to them. They do not know how to interact with nor do they understand the new you. Your growth rattles the cages of their own buried issues and pushes them out of their comfort zones. Your evolution is a mirror into which friends and family may not be ready to look. Send them love and stay on your path. Like everyone else, including ourselves, they will only look into their own mirror of truth when they are ready.

The Spirit Warrior is not deluded, for even the strongest person cannot pull everyone else to safety. As a Spirit Warrior you will shout encouragement and demonstrate strength through your actions.

You no longer have the need to make others wrong nor will you see yourself as superior or inferior. You have no need to defend or justify your actions.

The Spirit Warrior simply goes within and walks the path without self-righteousness or judgment of those who choose a different path.

Ultimately, we are each responsible for swimming to shore ourselves. As a Spirit Warrior you will forge ahead with your own mission because what other people think of you is none of your business. Rather than trying to fix or solve other people's issues, you now simply detach from people who choose a path that conflicts with yours.

You will learn more about detachment in an upcoming lesson, but here is the basic idea. Detaching and moving forward are two of the many difficult things you will do on your new journey. Leaving behind friends and people you love, no matter how strong you become, will trigger that old sense of guilt and make you question whether you should keep trying to pull them along with you. Leaving behind people you never imagined or intended to leave behind is painful. Giving up someone you love because you love yourself unconditionally is a very difficult process; especially when that other person clings tightly or lashes out at you. These reactions from others may trigger your own deepest fears.

Stick with your own process. Love yourself through the process. Some days you will be strong and other days you will slip back to old patterns. Love yourself on the up days and on the down days. Remind yourself that you are learning and forging authentic power not in a single flash of magic, but rather moment-by-moment, choice-by-choice, day-by-day over time. Strive not to judge yourself or others. Just keep moving forward. The minutes and hours of peace and freedom will start to add up and slowly turn into days. Then you will experience entire weeks that are peaceful. Weeks gradually turn into months and eventually years. Ultimately, you create a lifetime of peace. Then one day it will hit you just how far you have traveled and who you have become. Moment by moment, choice by choice, you've created a new you.

As you get healthier, there will probably be a natural settling and filtering process. Some of your old friends and family will choose to embrace the new you and join you on your path. Some will not. Some relationships will burn away in an instant from the heat of your clarity. The people with whom you used to get high or drunk will not recognize or understand the new you. They will vanish from your reality and you from theirs. Certain boyfriends and girlfriends will simply not make sense for you, either, if they do not embrace your path and take responsibility for theirs as well.

Other relationships won't end or change overnight, but in a more gradual way. Spouses and family members will eventually either embrace or turn away from your path. They may choose to take responsibility for their own lives as well, and they may not. Your truth will lead everyone in your life to the still waters and the reflection of their own reality. And if they don't take responsibility for what they see, you may choose to end the relationship or set strong new boundaries to protect your growing freedom.

You will also observe a steady reconnection with some of your old friends and a gradual drift away from others. If friends choose to join you on your new path, those relationships will begin anew from a better place and flourish on a new foundation of truth and honesty. If others choose to stay behind, that is their choice and not your responsibility. We each choose our own lives and experiences. You will undoubtedly begin attracting healthier new friends, business associates and romantic partners on your journey as well. You are creating a new reality with exciting possibilities that simply did not exist for you previously.

Eventually it will get easier and easier for you to detach from people and situations that disrupt your sacred inner peace. As a Spirit Warrior, you love yourself too much to stay around stuck people. Now you simply bless them with love and let them go. It's not cold or ruthless or selfish; detaching and taking care of yourself is actually loving both yourself and others. You are taking responsibility for stopping old patterns that create chaos and pain. The healthier you get, the sooner you will detach from unhealthy people. Now, rather than starting relationships with unhealthy people, you will gradually stop attracting those people into your life. And when they do cross your path, you will easily move among and around them without engaging them and disturbing your peace. You will even silently bless them with the intention that they, too, are able to find their peace. You become a force of love in the world rather than fear, and love is what you will share.

As a Spirit Warrior, you are learning to take care of yourself and stop looking to others for what you must find within. Solitude gives you the space to explore your inner terrain. As a Spirit Warrior, you embrace your shining light. From this place, not only will you choose not to hurt yourself or others, you will be unable to do so.

In your new alone time you will discover a deeper feeling of connection: You are connected to the power that created you.

And when you become less needy, almost as if by magic, you attract friends, lovers and spouses who are also less needy and therefore able to give and receive freely. You love and give to others because you want to share the joy you already know in your heart, not because you feel empty and alone and need someone else to fill your inner void. Ultimately, all of your relationships improve when you embrace uncertainty and being alone and learn to find your own highest and best inside.

Are you ready to step into uncertainty and embrace being alone?

In what loving ways will you nurture and soothe yourself?

How will you connect with yourself in healthy ways in your alone time?

Again, taking a few days to write down and share your answers with others is a powerful demonstration of your commitment to transformation.

4

Embrace your own death.

Listen close because you are already dead. We're all dead.

Not literally, but whether today or tomorrow or forty years from now, you will one day be dead. You will then be buried or burned into ash and that will be the end of your Earthly existence. Death is real. Death is inevitable. Death awaits you.

Do not be afraid.

What may strike you initially as a negative or morbid thought is simply a truth many of us deny. As a Spirit Warrior, you no longer deny or sugarcoat truth. You let the truth stand as it is without judgment. Death is a truth that is neither good or bad; death just is. Death is a process in your evolution. Your body dies and frees your infinite spirit. For the life well-lived, death is a reward.

For you, as a Spirit Warrior, death is a truth you accept and embrace. In visualizing your own death you find your real life. As a Spirit Warrior, you know the folly of trying to make something go away by simply not talking about it. We human beings don't want to talk about our mortality, but in fact, not talking about our own impending death only allows our fears to silently grow. And then we distract ourselves from the real issue, that unspoken fear and knowledge that in the end we all die.

There is no death of what is real
Because what is real is infinite
And infinity is an ocean of peace
That we can all know within
Before we leave this Earth.
And when we know we can share with others,
Not to tell them the path,
But to be a droplet of light from that infinite ocean
So that they, too, may find their way.

This is an important lesson in becoming a Spirit Warrior. Close your eyes now and begin to imagine your own death. Feel it. Breathe it in and allow yourself to experience the end of your Earthly life. What are your final thoughts? As your last breath draws nigh, what has your life meant? Who are you and what are you leaving behind as you progress forward? As you get ready to leave, what is important and what is not?

By experiencing your own death in this way, you are knocking on the door of your highest Self and spirit. You are cutting through all the cultural clutter and chatter to the pure spirit that is you, that perfect, unchanging energy waiting to be rediscovered; that cosmic and infinite essence that will survive the death of your physical body. Who is that energy that is timeless, boundless and pure potential? You may have forgotten, but you are right there on the other side of that door if you will just knock and then listen to what you hear. Then you are literally communing with your creator—God, the Universe, spirit, infinity—whatever you choose to call the nameless source, and asking the real questions.

What do I need to know?

How can I best serve in this lifetime?

What is my life to mean when I am gone from this planet?

How might my life change if I embraced death every day?

As a Spirit Warrior you now see the truth: Who you are and your worth are inherent and intact just because you are you. Let this truth soak in and allow yourself, perhaps, to truly relax for the first time because there is nothing more to do. Nothing more to accomplish, attain or acquire to make it all right. Just be with yourself now and experience that simple joy.

This chapter is short because all you have to do is choose to let go and see what your own death can show you. Enter your own death, accept death, embrace death. Rather than waiting for actual death, make some practice runs. Begin a spiritual conversation with your own death. Invite your death to sit beside you in your mental sweat lodge. Then listen closely and let your death teach you about how to live.

With this lesson especially, take some days to ponder and embrace your own death before moving on to the next lesson.

What can your death teach you?

5

Examine your concept of the spiritual realm.

Unexamined ideas and beliefs about the nature of the Universe, God and religion are usually those passed onto us by parents, teachers, friends and other well-meaning people. We may choose to embrace these same ideals, but the Spirit Warrior is not truly free without looking inside and examining the origin and nature of beliefs. As a Spirit Warrior, you choose your own reality. Even if what you choose as your spiritual base is what you've long believed, you will be acting from a place of choice and self responsibility.

> *Please take me deeper,*
> *Great Spirit Guide,*
> *Into that unfathomable*
> *Place of peace*
> *To live forever.*

Regardless of what you choose to call the infinite and unseen, there exists a life-force energy that connects everything. All that we see in the world of form—solid shapes, buildings, people, trees—is actually an illusion of molecules and space bound together by this mysterious energy. Any quantum physicist will confirm this new perspective of reality's core. It is the same energy within every living creature and object in the Universe. The same energy that binds your cells to form tissue, muscle and bone, is the same energy that opens flowers at dawn and makes planets revolve around the sun. Uncovering your spirituality is about opening yourself and connecting to that unseen life force that binds everything together.

The spirituality you choose as an adult may be very different from what you learned as a child. As a Spirit Warrior you may gravitate back to or away from traditional religious practices. You may struggle with believing any concept of spirituality, God and the unseen. Start with what you can believe: we know the Universe is limitless and infinite. Scientists know that our Universe is expanding. We also know scientifically that there are numerous unseen forces at work in our Universe.

Rather than thinking of God as being 'out there',
just try embracing the unseen energy
and the mystery of life.

What force is moving the clouds?
What makes your heart beat?
And who is doing all this thinking about what force is moving the clouds and what
makes your heart beat?

You may be surprised at the answer.

For example, the pull of gravity simultaneously anchors everything to the Earth's surface. This is pure energy: we cannot see or touch or taste the magnetic energy of gravity. We cannot access gravity through the use of any of our five senses. We can only point to its effects as evidence of its existence.

Love is an unseen energy: we cannot examine love under a microscope. We cannot scientifically prove love exists at all yet we know love is real because we know and feel its effects. The love we have for our partners, families and friends is not something tangible.

Whether love or gravity or creative ideas you create during your dreams, much of our reality is unseen energy at work. This force is everywhere around you, throughout the Universe, and it is also within you. You are not separate from the energy that created you; you are that same energy. God, if that is what you call the universal energy, is not out there and separate from you; God *is* you and around you simultaneously. You are that same pure spirit energy. Without this unseen energy—the life force—you would be a lump of bone and tissue.

In terms of mystery, we know that our Earth hurtles through space completely contained in an atmosphere that provides the exact amount of sunlight, water and oxygen to support human life. Yet every other planet in this solar system is barren and without a protective atmosphere. And on this single planet are billions of people past and present each genetically unique. Is that not the ultimate mystery?

Twelve-step programs tap into this notion of an unseen higher power or synergy that exists when people come together to share their triumphs and struggles.

The whole is greater than the sum of its parts. This same energy force is what you feel at church, or at a packed stadium or at a rock concert. The collective energy of people gathering for a common cause is not something you can access with your five senses. Yet, belief and energy are at work in the unseen realm.

Trying to define or label or put a structure around the life force and unseen universal intelligence is not necessary. In our quest for understanding, human beings have created tens of thousands of different God concepts. But in truth, there is only the One, regardless of what we choose to call this cosmic force. And we are all connected and unified to the One even though our egos cling to the notion that we are separate from each other.

As a Spirit Warrior, you seek to move away from the illusion of ego and connect with the infinite flow of invisible sustenance. The Spirit Warrior is not concerned with attempts to label, define or categorize this infinite force.

The Spirit Warrior simply practices acceptance, surrender and trust of all that is and all that will be.

The Spirit Warrior sees that when we attempt to define and label something we place yet another human interpretation, that is, a structure we can comprehend, around that which is truly infinite.

In your spiritual quest, there is no need to make anyone else's view or religion wrong. Religious fundamentalism that creates fear and hurts others is obviously not the work of spirit, but rather ego. Keep your focus on spirituality and truth and love. The Spirit Warrior is interested only in knowing the benevolent truth of the Universe. You will find the path that works for you. Free others to find their paths. Send out love and unity rather than hate and fear.

LISTEN—Be still, meditate and ask, "How may I best serve for the highest good?"

RECEIVE—Pay attention. Watch for the synchronicities that begin to appear with regularity.

ACT—Faith without works is dead. Trust and follow the guidance you receive.

Step within and quiet yourself. Seek to cool the present-moment fires in your mind, the blaze that scorches inner peace in a flash of searing heat when we don't stop to listen and follow our own inner voice and highest guidance. Seek to put aside instant gratification. Focus on connecting to something that will quench the thirst in your soul. Find your personal ways of tuning into your spirit whether meditation, prayer and ritual, finding solitude, journaling, being in nature, creative arts and hobbies, or yoga. There are hundreds of others. Find the ways that work for you.

Become like a child in your quest for truth and be open and flexible. Become curious about the mystery of the Universe in which we find ourselves. Move from the rigid place in your mind that says this spiritual stuff is nonsense. You can choose to be open to the possibility of an infinite intelligence working in the Universe. Simply be willing to believe in something that connects us all and is both outside us and within us simultaneously.

How do you define your spirituality?
Through fear? Or love?

What new, or traditional, rituals will you begin practicing around your spirituality?

How can you incorporate this into your other new patterns—loving yourself,
gratitude, forgiveness and surrender?

6

Pick up the powerful spiritual practice of detachment.

As a Spirit Warrior, you are learning to be eternally vigilant against any person, place or situation that may disturb your sacred inner peace. As mentioned, detachment becomes one of the most powerful tools on your spiritual odyssey. When done lovingly, detachment is healthy to both yourself and others because you choose to no longer participate in chaos, drama and unhealthy situations. From a Zen perspective, detachment is the practice of non-doing wherein you accomplish everything by simply detaching and, in essence, doing nothing.

The Spirit Warrior who no longer drinks alcohol because it was a self-destructive pattern chooses to detach from the friends, bars, nightclubs and parties that foster excessive drinking.

The Spirit Warrior who has a pattern of choosing unhealthy men for her relationships detaches from men who themselves are not on the path of spirituality and conscious living.

The Spirit Warrior who finds it difficult to relate to people stuck in old patterns chooses to detach and focus on being his best rather than trying to convince them to change.

The intention behind detachment is key. Detachment is not about making other people wrong or being self-righteous about your own path. Detachment is a loving act because you demonstrate respect by freeing yourself and others to be. We are each free to choose our own path. Detachment says, "I love you and I love myself so I am going to pursue my spiritual path, and I free you to pursue yours." Basically, if the two paths should merge again then that will be wonderful, and if they do not that will be wonderful in a different way. Detachment is about letting go of control.

The Spirit Warrior essentially chooses not to rescue nor do you expect anyone to rescue you. The Spirit Warrior says NO when you mean NO without shame or guilt. The Spirit Warrior speaks clearly about what you want and need from others, and you ask what others want and need from you. The Spirit Warrior does not step in with unsolicited help, but reminds others that you will do what you can when asked.

All of your conscious living and detachment is probably going to stir things up in your personal relationships with friends, family, partners and work peers.

The Spirit Warrior does not fear rejection. Rejection is impossible when you are grounded in Spirit.

People who react negatively to your growth are actually rejecting themselves. Your growth becomes a painful mirror for people who are still getting ready to be free.

Your truth and path are valid and intact regardless of what others choose. You are you with them, without them, with good reactions, with bad reactions. Nothing anyone does changes your truth. As a Spirit Warrior you speak your truth to validate you for *you* and not anyone else. Spirit Warrior, now is the time to begin owning yourself and let others own themselves.

Are there any people from whom you need to detach? Are there any objects or behaviors from which you need to detach?

Make a list in your journal. Share your list with a trusted friend.

7

Create a celebration for your fears and invite them all.

A Spirit Warrior does not run from fear. Instead, a Spirit Warrior invites fear into your sacred inner circle to celebrate. When you do so, you realize that fear is not the big, scary monster you created in your mind. When you begin observing your fears, what you find is often vague phantoms and projections about the anticipation of some future pain. Amid the drumbeat of now, fear often vanishes.

And yet the unchallenged fears in our minds have controlled us for so long that what started as tiny thoughts have grown into terrifying beasts with the power to destroy us. Like *The Wizard of Oz*, when we peek behind the curtain, we discover that our fears have been using smoke and shadows all these years to deceive us. We learn that our fears have no real power unless we choose to let fear control us.

The Spirit Warrior also has empathy for the fears you discover because fear becomes a tool; fear is an emotion the Spirit Warrior embraces and uses. The Spirit Warrior begins a conversation with fear and asks the fear what message it brings for every emotion brings us a message for action. Being fully alive and human means experiencing the wide spectrum of emotions whether pleasurable or painful. Fear is one of the common emotions we will experience.

Everyone feels fear. The Spirit Warrior, however, uses fear as the fire to ignite transformation.

Fear becomes a useful servant by indicating what you need to change and how you need to prepare yourself.

As a Spirit Warrior, you begin to ask, "What would happen if I decided to acknowledge and then let go of all my fears?" Like choosing to be free and stepping off the cliff inside yourself, letting go of fear happens in an instant.

Begin your celebration. Make your list of every fear and then invite them into the light. Fear of not being loved. Fear of not being good enough. Fear of being insignificant. Fear of being abandoned. Fear of looking stupid. Fear of death. Fear of money. Fear of success. Fear of failure.

When you see yourself reduce your fear by confronting it rather than running, then you are ready to step into the fear and allow the fear to be around you. You will see that fear serves you as an indicator of your growth and expansion. As a Spirit Warrior, you see that fear protects and guides you. You get to the other side when you adopt the tools of acceptance, surrender and trust around your fears.

Perhaps loved ones will not be able to understand or support your journey. You are scared because the fear is real and can be quite terrifying. You are in a battle for the freedom of your own mind. By simply stepping on the path, you are already winning the battle. But the fear will tell you otherwise. The fear will deceive you and tell you the old way is safer. If nothing else, the old way is certainly more familiar. These deceptions cast by your fears are what keep you stuck where you do not want to be. Feel the fear of losing people you love and proceed on your path with self-love. Feel the fear of giving up what you thought was real and proceed on your path with determination. Feel the fear of releasing the old patterns that have always comforted you, and proceed on your path with courage.

Now, as a Spirit Warrior, you are going to confront the Demon Fear that is greater than all your other fears combined—
Stepping into your potential and being your best Self.

Surprisingly, nothing will send the Spirit Warrior scurrying for cover faster than uncovering your best and brightest. A paradox, indeed. As you progress on your path, you are going to reveal a rare treasure that has been buried inside you. Be prepared as you scrape the dirt away and push aside the lid because the brilliance that shines forth can be terrifying. You are tapping into something sacred and real, which is the core of who you are meant to be, your life purpose, and all your wonderful talents and genius. We can intellectually discuss the universal energy, God, and life force, but when you discover your celestial light and experience loving unity firsthand, a normal reaction is immense fear.

Do not fear if, after leaving behind self-destructive ways and enjoying new successes in your life, you suddenly find yourself doing things you thought you were done doing. Do not fear if you start doing, or not doing, things to sabotage your own wonderful new ways of living. This is a normal fear reaction to uncovering your potential. This type of fear will show up in many ways:

• You're finally succeeding in a real way, and you start eating the old comfort foods again. Or you get a powerful urge to drink or do drugs or retreat to whatever used to make you feel safe and comfortable.

• You've learned to set healthy boundaries and detach from relationships that caused you pain, and you suddenly find yourself wanting to call an old lover. Or you allow yourself to get pulled into a relationship with someone you know is not healthy for you.

• You start making the income you've always wanted, and you find yourself procrastinating, not returning calls and thinking about how not to lose what you have rather than continuing to go after your new abundance.

• You start to feel deeply connected spiritually through your new rituals and fellowship and you find yourself acting out sexually and saying things like, "I've been doing so well. This just came out of the blue."

• You start a new workout routine, change your eating habits, and love your shrinking waistline. And then you find yourself missing workouts, over-eating or picking up cigarettes again.

What's going on in these scenarios? When you start to be the person your soul wants you to be, it's terrifying. In fact, it's more terrifying than being stuck. Being a conscious, purposeful person creates all sorts of uncertainty, change, movement and growth, which triggers fear.

We know that all human beings use patterns. We pick up our most effective old patterns again and again because initially they work so effectively. The problem, however, is that unresolved emotions—fear, anger, guilt, shame—do not go away simply because we numb them with our old ways.

In fact, the unresolved emotions start to stack up inside us. Not facing something will never make it go away; not facing our emotions only creates more pain that we will eventually have to confront. And if we do not face ourselves, the emotions come out as self-destructive patterns, anxiety and physical illness in the body. As you understand your patterns and release them, you create an unexpected fear: Being Free.

Freedom means no more hiding from yourself.

Freedom means accepting everything as it is and leaving behind the old, lonely terrain into which you used to retreat.

Freedom means, perhaps, leaving old friends and loved ones behind as you cross the bridge into a new world of clarity.

Freedom means just being, and just being, ultimately, is the place where serenity, reverence, love and profound knowing of yourself reside.

Freedom means letting go of everything you used to think was real in order to fulfill your potential.

This is all very new and, therefore, creates fear. The Spirit Warrior understands that all change, even good change, brings with it new stress and fear. The first step is to go back to Lesson #1: Love yourself when you don't do it perfectly. Love yourself regardless of your mistakes and zigzags and be thankful you are so much more aware now.

Choose now to not punish yourself anymore for the mistakes you've made. Love yourself for your progress and resolve to do better today. Start fulfilling your potential and be aware and ready for the new set of fears that will start cropping up.

Will family and friends reject me if I change?

When I truly succeed will I be alone?

These are difficult and painful truths for the Spirit Warrior to face. And the answer to each is, YES, some may reject you, and you may leave behind others. It may be one of the consequences of freeing yourself. But the flip side is that if *everyone* chose to free themselves, no one would be left behind.

You can only free yourself and encourage others to do the same.

When you free yourself, you change the world because you start leading by example.

Allow the fear to be there as you evolve and find your true potential and purpose. Do not let the new fear of success derail your journey. Use all the tools and discipline you have learned to allow yourself to flourish. Feel all those fear thoughts, new and old, and keep marching forward on your path.

Each day the Spirit Warrior asks, "What brings me the most fear?" And then you wait for the answer, which usually comes quickly if you are ready to listen. And when you receive the answer, acknowledge those things that bring the most fear. Thank the fear for protecting you. And then tell the fear you are going to move forward.

The goal is not to banish or push away all your fears. Facing fear, acknowledging fear, embracing fear as your guide; these are the way of the Spirit Warrior. Here are some ideas to begin embracing your fears:

GREET YOUR FEAR: Do not allow fear or any other emotion to send you running to escape into old comfort patterns. Remember, the old patterns don't work. Nor should we try to deny our fears. Simply acknowledge and identify the emotion: Okay *fear, I see. Yes, I'm feeling fear about...*That's all. No more running. No more hiding. Just greet the fear and then let it be there with you. It won't bite.

BE THANKFUL: When you greet a fear or fears as they show up, be thankful for the emotion. The fear is trying to tell you something. Acknowledge the fear by saying, *Thank you for showing up in my life to protect me and alert me to some potential danger. I hear your message.*

BE STILL: Allowing your fear (as well as your sadness, hurt, anger, joy, passion and all your other emotions) to simply be with you is a powerful step. Rather than emotions dictating your actions, you will now embrace the emotion and just let it be. Fear has no magical power over you unless you choose to give it that power. When you run away to escape at the first sign of fear, you give your power over to the fear. Just be still and breathe.

BE CURIOUS: Many fears, after you embrace them, will quickly dissolve away. Others will linger. Either way, now you are in a much more resourceful place to explore the fear. Ask yourself: *What are you trying to tell me?* You will uncover some fears as completely unfounded. You can choose to let those go with, *Thank you for showing up in my life, and I am going to feel this fear and proceed.*

Other fears may signal a specific course of action: *Hey, you've got that big presentation next week so you'd better start preparing.* That fear is giving you a useful message. You can thank this fear in the same way and begin preparing. The Spirit Warrior finds genuine power not in conquering fear, but rather embracing your fears, allowing them to be, and then having a conversation with the fear. Begin now:

What are your fears? Write your list in your journal.

Are you willing to invite them into your sacred sweat lodge for a conversation?
Are you ready to free yourself of your fear by finding out what your fear is telling you?
Are you willing to reduce your fear by doing the things you fear most?

Once you have your list of fears and answers to these questions, what are you committed to doing in the next fifteen minutes to confront and reduce your fear?

8

Embrace now as the only true reality.

As a Spirit Warrior, you see the illusion of time. This moment is the only reality we have. Any other projection of time, whether past or future, is part of the dream we create in our minds. The past is gone like vapor except when we keep it alive; the future, too, is just an image we project. And of all the resources we may or may not have—money, genetics, education, upbringing, intelligence, physical abilities—time is the only one that is equal to us all. Each of us gets to choose how we will use the moment.

The Spirit Warrior understands that now is the day to be free. Now is the day to allow all the love and spirit energy of the Universe to flow through you. Now is the day to create, love and laugh. Now is the only time to accept who you are one hundred percent and surrender to your larger purpose. Now is the moment to choose to set yourself free.

Pay attention to today. Right now. Each moment. Each experience. Each breath. Savor it. Enjoy. Feel. There is nowhere to go. There is nothing to become. You are already here with yourself. Here are some ways to live more in the moment:

CLEAN UP YOUR PAST: All the great spiritual traditions promote forgiveness. In the twelve-step tradition you make a list of the people you've harmed, including yourself, before you became conscious and aware. Once you have the list, then do what you can to make amends and clean up the garbage you left on the trail. You don't need to further punish yourself. Just go back and do what you can to make amends without judgment or shame. Begin a process of forgiveness to release old, toxic emotions. You also need to resolve any traumas or issues that may still be controlling your behavior today. You may want to seek a good therapist to assist you in this work. Before you find forgiveness and make amends, you will always be dragging around the past. Whether consciously or unconsciously, your past misdeeds and unresolved emotions will gnaw at your peace and greatly diminish your ability to stay in the now.

Are you ready to be free?

If you are, then summon your courage and begin this important clearing work.

STAY OUT OF THE FUTURE: The Spirit Warrior creates reality by having a clear vision of the life you intend. But spending too much time in some imaginary future fantasy drains your authentic power. Your only power to create and act is now. Let go of the future and how it will unfold. Focus instead on what you need to do today, this hour, this moment. In so doing, you are participating in life with a sense of trust that as you do what you need to do, things will work out as they should. You simply focus on now and allow the Universe to handle the details.

Are you ready to move out of the future and take responsibility for doing what you need to do right now?

MEDITATE DAILY: A powerful method for grounding yourself is getting quiet once or twice a day. Our lives and world and minds are full of constant noise and chatter. Everywhere you go there is a constant din of external noise and clutter. Add to that the unceasing rush of internal noise—thoughts, fear, anxiety, worry, endless TO DO lists—that plow through the mind from the moment we awake to the time we go to sleep. Meditation is simply a quiet rest stop from the world wherein you transcend the illusion. Meditation connects you back to reality and grounds you there. The Spirit Warrior takes this proactive step and carves out the time to experience the bliss of being.

When you quiet the mind you access that highest spirit part of yourself. You learn to find joy and bliss and happiness in the immediate moment just by experiencing your aliveness. Sitting quietly and observing your breath reminds us that being alive is enough; nothing else truly matters.

There are hundreds of ways to meditate and entire books on meditation and many excellent CDs devoted to the subject. Your mission as a Spirit Warrior is to find the way that works best for you. Whether through yoga, transcendental meditation, chanting, or sitting under your favorite tree every morning, whatever works best for you is the right way. Simply sitting for ten minutes and observing your breath can be very cleansing. Meditation does not have to be complicated or daunting.

List all the new ways you will stay grounded in the present.
Are you committed to these new practices?
Or are you still waiting for someone or something outside yourself
to set you free?

YOUR SACRED QUEST—

This concludes Part Two of your Spirit Warrior training. Your test question is the same:

The Big Question:
Are you ready to be free, or are you still getting ready to be free?

Points to Ponder

• At the core of your work is changing those dusty old beliefs and creating powerful new internal knowledge based on truth. Here, now, are affirmations distilled from Parts One and Two. Remember, repetition is the key to conditioning new patterns. What appears smooth and effortless—a drum solo, a fluid golf swing, an articulate and entertaining presentation—became so through thousands and thousands of repetitions. Continue to use repetition and discipline, now with awareness, to become the person you will be tomorrow.

From Part One…
1. I love and accept myself, and I am free.
2. I forgive myself and all others, and I am free.
3. I choose to create miracles right now, and I am free.
4. I choose peace, and I am free.
5. I release all old patterns, and I am free.
6. I surrender and ask for help, and I am free.

From Part Two…
I surrender to and embrace my truth.
I am free to rebel against old patterns and beliefs.
I now embrace uncertainty and my alone time.
I accept, embrace and welcome my death.
I am uncovering my own spirituality.
It is okay for me to detach with love.

I embrace my fears and trust the messages fear brings me.
I embrace this moment as the only true reality.

• Are you ready to love yourself now? Or do you need more time?

• Are you willing to believe in what might be possible for you rather than what you think you already know?

• What is your vision of yourself being successful? Capture this vision in your journal.

• Are you taking time each day to practice affirming and loving yourself? Are you continuing to forgive yourself and others each day? Write down some more ways you can affirm your highest Self and share your discoveries with a friend.

• Are you willing to just surrender? Or do you need more time?

PART III

Your return home

1

Trust. Step off the cliff

You are on your path. You are doing much work in learning to love yourself and choosing to be free. You are seeking others who also want to be free. You are willing to face and release your old patterns that no longer serve you. You are learning to embrace your own death each day as a way to distill your life and true purpose into brilliant clarity. You are facing your fears and practicing detachment. You are grounding yourself through meditation. Now, in this lesson, you are going to go through an initiation of sorts. All the work you are doing has brought you to an important mental and emotional precipice.

You are going to become a Spirit Warrior.

You are ready to be free.

You are going to simply let go.

> *You are standing, Spirit Warrior, at the edge of the highest of all cliffs,*
> *that place inside you that contains the blackest abyss of your deepest fears.*
> *As a Spirit Warrior, you are ready to peer into the darkness and*
> *step off into the unknown.*

> *Becoming free happens in an instant. Like a flash of brilliant lightning,*
> *you simply say, "I am ready to be free."*

You may have been here before. Fear held you back. Doubt held you back. Anxiety held you back. Feeling unworthy of success and undeserving of the life you want held you back. You are stronger now. You are ready to be free once-and-for-all. You step off the cliff. At first, you will not know whether you will sprout wings and fly. You fall through darkness. You know you cannot go back. Release yourself. This is where you face your fears. This is where you feel your feelings. This is where you let the pain wash over you. This is where you stop running and simply let go. You embrace this freefall into the unknown as a necessary step to freedom.

71

Stepping off the Cliff

You have to go away, Spirit Warrior, into yourself. Alone. Pain. Falling. Blackness all around. Your old Self is dying. You are saying good-bye, forever, to the old ways. Feeling so alone. Embrace the pain and emptiness of the old Self dying for death is freedom. Your heart sings your beauty and spirit. Your spirit touches your soul. You are dying to be reborn. Death is so scary. And yet so peaceful. You ease your grip. Your heart is pure. You are everywhere. And nowhere. You whisper your love, and you know you hear.

Do not fear: Spirit sees you. Be still. You are so close. Let go. You're safe. Breathe. This is the place. Feel the quiet all around. Welcome home. Fear no more. You walked across the chasm not alone, but alone with you. The love is around you and in you. You are more than the pain of coming home. You are you. Love and Light.

You flash across the Universe and back to whence you came. The answer is in your heart. You are the answer to every question ever asked. You are one with all the love now. All of the love in the Universe is one single drop of beauty in the endless ocean of love inside you now. Cling no more to another's love for you are LOVE.
Be still. Be the love. Let the tears of joyous release and celebration be your companion now. The pain is no more.

As a Spirit Warrior, trust is stepping off the cliff. Through simple acceptance, surrender and trust, you will tap an undiscovered power within yourself.

Don't believe the thought—Trust the feeling.

Create a clearing for your own *satori*, or going through the gate, to manifest. Create a place of true surrender, willingness and ask for spiritual guidance. Simply lean into and allow your pain to take you where you need to go. No running from the pain, no medicating the pain, no resisting the pain. To be free, simply surrender and become willing.

A new adventure, a magical trip
Through a purple doorway into my soul.
No one can come. Not even her or him.
No one. Except me.

I relax my grip and fall through the black.
A wave rises up and catches me,
Soothes me. Peace all around.
I am home with myself.
Darkness fades. The Light says Hello.

I am willing.
I surrender. Please show me the way.
What is my mission? My purpose?
Who shall I be?

I trust I am at the doorway to my soul.
I am willing to step through
And be.
Simply be what I am to be.

When you step through the gate, you will sense a peace unlike any you have ever felt. A deep stillness that we often seek in so many things external. This sense of wholeness is simply a return to what you have always been: pure love. You will not think about this peace as in 'I am so peaceful.' Rather, you will feel this peace as a deep inner calm. Many of the old nagging emotions will quietly dissolve in the light when you step through and be with your highest Self. The emotions that do not serve you, but which were at one time ever-present, cannot survive the light of truth. You will sense an odd absence of worry, doubt, fear, loneliness, anxiety, mistrust, sadness, hurt, anger, resentment and cynicism. The freedom of no longer needing these emotions as a divide within yourself will open your soul to freely express your divinity. Going through the gate happens in an instant just as a clogged pipe can open after being completely blocked. In one moment the liquid is unable to pass through the clog, and in the next moment the flow is restored to one hundred percent capacity. Just because the flow returns in an instant does not mean we doubt it.

Nor should we doubt the return to our divinity, our own inner flow, because it happens quietly, in a single moment, without any fanfare or painful, lifelong struggle. We are each free, or not free, through our choices and intentions. We can choose freedom in an instant, right now, or choose to remain clogged and suffer. Suffering, if nothing else, is familiar. And it is very seductive to be attached to what is familiar.

To many, this way of deep trusting will seem completely foreign and out of the realm of possibility. Even religious people or people in recovery with many years of sobriety from their old addictions will be skeptical and unable to accept the possibility of *satori*, of reaching a place within where one simply knows that she or he will never again choose the old behavior. Not now, not today, not ever. This knowing comes not from an attitude of control and conquering because fear disempowers people and weakens the spirit. This deeper knowing and trusting emanates from a sacred place of reverence, surrender and humility. That which you love unconditionally, including yourself, you can no longer hurt. Love, indeed, conquers all.

We each must simply choose our path. Whatever path works for *you* is your best path. Being willing to believe in the possibility of *satori*, or instant awakening, is a deeper level of freedom. As a Spirit Warrior, you only have to decide what you choose to believe and then act on that belief. There is no need to convince others to see your light. Simply know and trust the light you find for yourself.

I left behind some old friends, for good,
And stepped through a new door
Into a Beingness that cannot fathom
Creating any more pain and suffering for Self or others.
We will make many great journeys
But none like this into the brilliance and love and
unchanging truth at our core.
The journey did not destroy us, never asking more
than we could take,
But always asking enough to bring us home.

And I looked back at those old friends
And smiled and cried and knew
That it was they who brought me home.
And then when I looked again
They were gone, and I knew I would
Never see them again, Ever, because they merged
Into the Love
Of infinity
To light the way
For others.

In reading this, you have already embarked on a sacred quest: Your true journey. Nothing is by chance. In an intricate dance of timing, possibility and purpose, you have been brought to this moment in this place to these words. To the uninitiated, this can be terrifying. Do not be afraid.

You are on your way home.

Are you willing to let go and let the cosmic spirit guide you?
Are you willing to step off the cliff and trust that you will know how to fly?

If you have never fully surrendered and are ready, then create a surrender ritual for yourself. You can light candles and pray. You can surrender through meditation. You can write your surrender in a journal or hike to the top of a mountain and surrender there. You can surrender at your support group. Go now, Spirit Warrior, and surrender. Now is the time. Simply let go and trust.

If you are not ready to surrender, then follow the same steps as above except just ask for guidance. Ask your highest Self to help you find the strength to let go. Go now, Spirit Warrior, and ask for your guidance. Now is the time. Simply let go and trust.

2

Pen your own Declaration of Independence.

Upon awakening, the Spirit Warrior greets the sunrise, quietly drives a stake in the ground and declares freedom. This is a choice you will make each day: The path of freedom (LOVE) or the path of distraction (FEAR). There are only the two paths.

On the path of love and truth, you are free of the illusory burdens of past and future. You are nurturing and integrating all your wonderful gifts, qualities, talents, dreams, abilities and serenity. You release what you cannot control and use your focus and energy to change what you can in healthy ways. You are writing your own Declaration of Independence.

From this day forward, you are no longer a victim, but rather a strong, powerful, emotionally-mature human being with the tools to live an authentic life based on your truth. From this day forward, you choose and promise to nurture those parts of yourself that have been seeking love and approval from external sources. Starting now, you find love and approval within yourself by connecting with your soul and highest Self. From now on, you promise to yourself that you will set healthy boundaries, assert your rights, needs and wants and do whatever you must to protect yourself emotionally. You declare that as of today, you are free to be you. Your step is lighter, your heart is serene and your spirit can soar because today you are reconnecting with a very special person, a miracle of the Universe: YOU!

Each day you are writing and living your own personal
Declaration of Independence.

As a Spirit Warrior, you become a person of integrity. First to yourself and then in all
your relationships with others.

Your new independence, Spirit Warrior, frees you from seeking. Rather than trying to get from your relationships, you are free to focus on giving. You are free to share the love overflowing from your heart. Paradoxically, focusing on giving love is what will bring more of the joy and love you need. The Spirit Warrior moves with a confidence and softness of power that keeps you grounded. This new core identity is who you have always been.

Now, write your own Declaration of Independence.

You can make it as long or as short as you'd like.
It could be two words—I'm Free!—or ten pages long. You decide.

You might include:
Your new boundaries, beliefs and affirmations, who you are and intend to be,
how you see the Universe now, what you will and will no longer accept, and
your grandest vision of yourself being successful.

Have Fun. Let the real YOU shine through in what you create.

And then, read your Declaration of Independence each day as a powerful affirmation
of who you intend to be.

Will you take the time now to affirm yourself in this new way? Or are you choosing to
skip over the actual work in order to get somewhere else? You have all the time in the
world. This book will wait for you. Your highest Self will wait for you.
Your transformation will wait for you.

You can plow ahead now or stay here with yourself.

You decide.

3

Find FLOW.

FLOW. We've all been there and experienced this magical state. FLOW happens in those moments when you experience a lightness and unity emanating from within even though you may be involved in a difficult or demanding task. You find this inner space when you are at your best and moving through an activity or the day's challenges with a pleasurable ease, clarity and joy.

Any hobby, sport or activity—even your work if you're lucky—will take you into FLOW. Without realizing it consciously, those old nagging twins of anxiety and fear quietly vanish. You are in the moment. The edges around 'what you are doing' and 'who you are' blur together. Time may become distorted and hours can pass in what, literally, feels like minutes. When you are in FLOW you lose your self consciousness and, paradoxically, you don't do this consciously. It just happens. FLOW is an altered state of reality, like being in a moving meditation or dance. In FLOW, the highest and best parts of you naturally shine through. Your talents and gifts rise to the surface. FLOW is the blissful zone in which the Spirit Warrior learns to spend more and more time.

Seeking FLOW, however, is tricky because the state occurs spontaneously and holistically rather than through some linear set of steps. In other words, that which you seek you cannot find, so rather than seeking FLOW, the Spirit Warrior focuses on being in the moment, being aware, and being conscious. That blissful feeling of FLOW will then occur spontaneously. However, just as soon as you say, "Wow, look, I'm in FLOW," you are no longer in FLOW.

FLOW is the beautiful butterfly that quietly lands on your shoulder while you're lost in the moment. Trying to chase and catch that same butterfly through effort, however, will prove futile. The FLOW that can be described in words is not the flow. You must be in the experience to have the experience. Simply know and trust you are in FLOW without needing to think. Notice and appreciate the butterfly and return your gaze within to your activity or stillness.

As a Spirit Warrior, one of the wonderful secrets you discover is that you can, to a large extent, choose how you feel. When you begin choosing and embracing empowering emotions—love, gratitude, passion, determination, contribution, confidence, curiosity—something magical happens: You begin to experience the FLOW state. You're in the groove. You get the mojo working. You're in that zone where everything just falls into place. You know the feeling because we've all been there (especially when we were children).

A Spirit Warrior also knows that like attracts like. This is a Universal Law. A Spirit Warrior chooses every day: The path of love, peace, connection, wealth and abundance. Or the path of distraction and spiritual death. And as you choose, so you create. You now have the power and freedom to carefully choose how to expend your daily supply of energy. In your old life, distractions chewed up much of your energy supply. Other people's issues, demands and chaos became your issues, demands and chaos. Your own challenges consumed your vital energy and then the disempowering coping strategies you chose further drained your spirit. When the energy was gone, there was none left for you to build a better life.

Now you walk a different path. In FLOW, there's a synergy whereby your energy actually increases through your alignment and congruency. Your energy is no longer being drained. In FLOW, you're plugged into an infinite energy supply, which is why kids (and adults, too!) can play for hours at high speeds without getting tired. Rather than fatigue, FLOW energizes.

When you enter this deep sense of peace and purpose in FLOW, regardless of what is happening in your external world, you are aligned and living with your highest Self. There is no way to describe exactly what being in FLOW feels like except to say you will know when you are there. And you will know when you are not as well.

Discovering how you experience FLOW is key. Perhaps it's a hobby or pursuit that gives you that feeling of connection and peace. Maybe it's a Sunday morning motorcycle ride either solo or with friends. Perhaps it's a physical pursuit such as yoga, Pilates or lifting weights. Maybe you find your FLOW in quieter activities like reading novels, morning walks or hiking. The Spirit Warrior who finds FLOW in their work is most fortunate. Being in FLOW and earning your income become one.

When do you feel your absolute best?

What activities or pursuits put you in that FLOW state of optimum experience?

How can you put yourself in FLOW every single day of your life?

BONUS: What do you want in this life? Have you given your all toward its attainment?

The Spirit Warrior knows winning is an internal game. What you give you get to keep. Being successful is not your income level or some other external achievement. Being successful is giving your all toward a worthy ideal or purpose, and in so doing, sharing your gifts with the world.

From this moment forward, your guidepost for whether you are being successful is internal, not external. Measure success by how much more of yourself you can give toward what you are doing right now. Only you will know when you are giving your all. The external scoreboard may indicate you are the game's winner, but if you have not given your all, you really did not win. Conversely, pouring your soul into a project one hundred percent—and thereby finding FLOW—makes you a success regardless of the external scoreboard. Externals come and go and include many factors that are out of our control: world events, business markets and cycles, stock market ups and downs, weather and many more. How much you give toward what you want, however, is one hundred percent your choice. The only person with the power to stop you from finding FLOW is you.

As a Spirit Warrior you are ready to allow your own success. On the old path the ego ruled the kingdom. The Spirit Warrior knows that true success is in relinquishing control to the energy that creates all. This change, this final casting off of the victim skin and identity, is scary because it is unchartered territory in the psyche. Being in FLOW is a surrender to where you are and what you are doing. Let go and trust the creative life force. It will take you where you need to be if you let it work for you. Choosing to create space into which your FLOW state can occur becomes a daily and powerful affirmation of your new power. Spirit Warrior, you are powerful beyond what you have allowed yourself to even imagine. Embrace your responsibility right now.

What are the ways you will find your FLOW every day?
List ten or more ways in your journal.

Once you've completed the list, take thirty minutes to go enjoy FLOW.
Pick one of your ways and immerse yourself in the activity.
Have the intention to let go and see where it leads you.

Don't analyze or interpret what's happening—just BE.

4

Create your own masterpiece.

Your work is almost complete. Actually, your work was complete before you began your search, before you began this book, before you were born. Read this sentence several times and let it sink in: *You have always been who you are.* All your fantastic voyages, your hero's journey, have really been about just remembering a simple truth, a truth you've always known. You are on the mandatory journey and also the journey not needed. In the end, it all comes back to you where your hero has been waiting for all of eternity.

Have you chosen to be free?

Have you done your work?

Are you now being the person your soul wants you to be?

Only you will know in your heart when the answer to each of these questions is a resounding YES. It matters not what anyone else's opinion is on this matter. You may deceive others, but never yourself. No one becomes a Spirit Warrior by reading someone else's words or by trying to live someone else's life. We must each take the necessary and oftentimes grinding actions to create the lives we want.

Your true Self will patiently wait, without judgment, for you to answer the questions above. And when you can shout **YES!** you will barely be able to contain your newfound joy, peace, enthusiasm and reverence for reality. You will have set yourself free, and there is no greater gift to yourself, to your loved ones, to the world. When one of us says **YES!** to our spirit, the world becomes a little brighter.

Once you are free your real adventure begins. But this will be a new type of adventure, often difficult, trying and demanding, but with an underlying lightness and freedom unlike the old ways. When you reach this place and know what you know, the Spirit Warrior gives away the key so as not to confuse the key with the knowing. If this book has been a helpful key, give it away freely. If loving yourself has been helpful, then love others freely. If getting ready to be free was helpful, then help others get ready to join you. If trusting yourself and the cosmic power is helpful, then continue to give that away by trusting. This is a journey, Spirit Warrior, with no beginning and no end. The journey not needed, the journey you cannot avoid.

> *The dreams you have are gifts from the Source.*
> *Life needs you to fulfill those dreams,*
> *Life needs you to succeed.*
> *Dreams pull you forward like a beacon*
> *Bringing you home to Infinity.*
> *Trust your own beacon*
> *For that is God showing you*
> *The Way.*

Beyond this Earthly life, your spirit energy will evolve into new possibilities. Being on the path means staying on the path because the old ways and demons and fears, no matter how strong and grounded you become, are infinitely patient and will continue to seduce you and call out to you. The Spirit Warrior stays strong through a new code:

> *Acceptance (especially of what we don't like or understand!)…*
> *Humility in all things…*
> *Strength through surrender and trust…*

Who We Are is the same as the power that created us. From your evolved place of knowing, Spirit Warrior, you are ready to create your own masterpiece. The canvas of your life is now blank.

> *When you step into Love you finally see*
> *That the Ocean of Tranquility was*
> *Never without, but within,*
> *Waiting for you, patiently waiting*
> *For your return.*

> *The moment of your return*
> *Moves the cosmic tumblers back into alignment*
> *And makes your love a part of Infinity*

So that others, too, can find their way.
Your Earthly life will never be the same for now you see
You are not of this Earth.

What masterpiece will you choose to create?

When you can freely give away the gifts you have discovered for yourself, you come full circle. This is the final step in the twelve-step tradition. This is *Love thy neighbor.* This is a life of service and meaning that can only come to fruition when you go inside and bring forth your gifts to the world. You alone may not cure cancer. You may not save the rain forests from destruction nor can you alone feed all the hungry people in the world. However, being your best is what the Universe most needs. Life found you for some specific purpose, and life needs you to share that purpose. When we each take responsibility for stopping the old patterns of chaos and pain and destruction and begin creating the lives we were each destined to create, we collectively change the world.

What you choose to do with this great power may seem trivial and insignificant against the backdrop of a planet with so many challenges. There is much pain and fear and confusion in the world, but that is only because people have drifted away from truth and spiritual connection. Fragmented minds create fragmented behaviors and consequences.

There is another movement afoot. People are rediscovering the truths you are finding and choosing to heal rather than hurt. People are rejecting the old mantra of 'More is better.' People are simplifying their lives. People are trading in material and external success markers and seeking spiritual meaning. People are talking about doing what truly matters. Men and women are choosing to become Spirit Warriors rather than victims.

The world is healing as we each heal ourselves. All of the world's ills would vanish in an instant if each individual rejected the stronghold of ego and instead chose the spiritual path of truth. Not self-righteous dogma or invoking the word *God* to control and dominate others through fear and force. The infinite voice of spirit resonates with the truth you have uncovered in these lessons and the power to create the life you want. Following the intelligent and universal voice of truth is in no way insignificant, Spirit Warrior.

Why do you suppose we as human beings revel in the great works past and present of architects, artists, musicians, sculptors and modern-day sports heroes? Why do we revere scientists, inventors and painters? Why do we knowingly suspend disbelief and enjoy live theatre and movies? What moves us at a symphony performance or rock concert?

In each instance we are vicariously celebrating that highest part of ourselves that we, perhaps, have not yet brought forth out of fear. We admire and connect with those creators who apparently, by some random stroke of the cosmic paint-brush, are given a gift and creative power to bring forth art, inventions, music and acts of physical prowess seemingly beyond our own grasp. But your highest and best is not beyond your grasp. You just have to find the courage to pick up the mantle and start trying. The Spirit Warrior knows the truth: we are each endowed with that same great and powerful ability to create.

The act of creation is simply tapping into the source energy.

We are each comprised of the same infinite energy that is in everything whether Shakespeare's quill, Picasso's paintbrush or the infinite energy that brought you forth and makes the planets revolve in our solar system.

All emanates from the One source.

We are quick to dismiss this notion of having that same power with beliefs such as *She is so creative* and *I've never been that creative.* But we each have the power to create albeit in wonderfully different ways. In fact, admiring the creativity in others and refusing to see our own is another way of choosing to be a victim.

What we will create is up to each of us. The creative arts and sports and inventing are more obvious manifestations of this energy. But so, too, are teaching, coaching, creating a business, finding solutions on a consulting basis, building and construction, fixing things, flying airplanes, ministry and volunteering. The ways in which we can manifest our individual creative abilities are infinite. Remember, you have the same ability to tap into creative energy that Einstein had. How you use it will be different, but it is the same energy whether you're creating a guitar solo or inspiring fourth graders.

This is your final lesson, Spirit Warrior, but your adventure has only just begun. Your lifelong mission now is to know what your mission is to be. When you accept the reality of your own impending death, you free yourself to find your purpose.

What does the still, growing voice of your spirit whisper to you
in your quiet moments?

If you knew you could not fail, what purpose would you acknowledge
in your heart?

If you knew you would be dead in one year, what purpose would you attempt to bring forth before your time on Earth is up?

If you're going to be dead anyway,
why not go do what your heart cries out to do?

Do not doubt any longer—know what you know. Do not fear your highest Self—embrace your truth. Do not run—simply be the light that shines from within. You are becoming, like those who have walked the path before you, a wiser, loving, future incarnation of yourself returning to this moment with the guidance, lessons and support for which you always yearned. You are developing a deep reverence for the joy, freedom and gratitude you now find in the simple moments of your life. You are stepping through the doorway into an infinite domain of freedom and possibility.

Becoming free is the greatest gift you can give yourself. And, paradoxically, the greatest gift you can give the world. The canvas is blank. The world awaits your gifts. Do not deprive us any longer of your highest and best. There remains only one question:

How will you share your greatness with the world?

Welcome to the tribe.
You are going to become a Spirit Warrior.

About the Author

Landon J. Napoleon picked up a pen at age ten and has been writing ever since. His touching debut novel *ZigZag* received widespread critical acclaim, found publishers in four countries, and went on to become a film starring Wesley Snipes and John Leguizamo. *The Spirit Warrior's Handbook* is Mr. Napoleon's first non-fiction book. He is based in Phoenix, Arizona.

0-595-33986-7

22053112R00064

Made in the USA
Lexington, KY
10 April 2013